Paris
An architectural guide

itineraries
5

Heinfried Wischermann

Paris
An architectural guide

arsenale et editrice

Heinfried Wischermann
PARIS
AN ARCHITECTURAL GUIDE

Design
Michela Scibilia

Translation from German
Steven Sidore

Photographs
Bernard Vedral
and
Heinfried Wischermann

Photo credits
Stefano Bianchetti, Paris
cover, p. 77, p. 109
Musée Carnavalet, Paris
da p. 11 a p. 17
Mark E. Smith, Venice
p. 87

Printed in Italy by
EBS Editoriale Bortolazzi-Stei
Verona

First edition
October 1997

© Copyright 1997
Arsenale Editrice srl

ISBN 88-7743-162-8

Contents

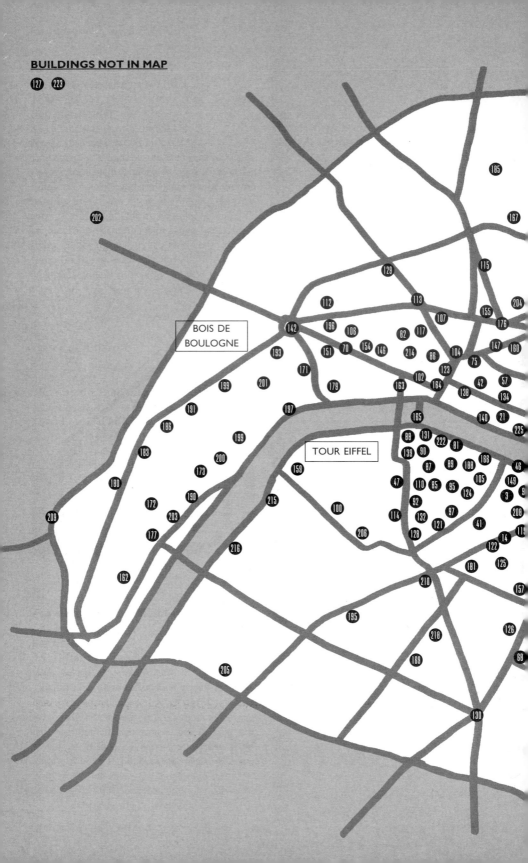

BUILDINGS NOT IN MAP

127 223

BOIS DE
BOULOGNE

TOUR EIFFEL

Introduction

Although Paris, the capital of the French Republic, does not lie in the geographic center of France, it is the political, economic, and cultural center of its country, more so than any other European capital. Paris is the headquarters of the French government, the National Assembly (Assemblée Nationale), the Senate, all judicial courts and ministries, all foreign embassies, and the greatest multitude of national and international organizations. Furthermore, Paris holds the headquarters of the Catholic Archdiocese, the Archdiocese of the Russian-Orthodox Church, the United Protestant Church of France, and the central organization for French Jews. The French higher educational system also revolves around Paris. Sorbonne is the oldest university in the country, and the Paris universities were all part of it until 1968 (they are now split into 13 divisions).

Paris is also one of the most heavily populated capitals in Europe. Although it occupies far fewer square miles than Berlin or London, it would take several weeks to view all of the sites explored in this book. Through careful planning, the city has even managed to maintain its own distinct character. With the addition of the Boulevard Périphérique in 1973, Paris reinforced its infrastructure of wide boulevards and civil cultivation—more so even than London. This is not to say that Paris is not changing. Because of the high rents and the permanent disarray of traffic in the older city sections, many residents have fled to the newer areas like Cergy-Pontoise, Evry, Marne-la-Vallée, Melun-Sénart, and Saint-Quentin-en-Yvelines, all of which have risen to prominence since the SDAURP (Schéma Directeur d'Aménagement et d'Urbanisme de la Région Parisienne report of 1965. These regions—Essonne, Hauts-de-Seine, Seine-et-Marne, Seine-

9

Saint-Denis, Val-de-Marne, Val-d'Oise, Yvelines–make up, with Paris, the lle-de-France (Région Parisienne), which, with over 10 million inhabitants in an area of only 12,008 square kilometers, is the 4th most populated region of its kind in the world. With the population predicted to reach 12 million by the year 2000, the infrastructure of this area is planned on a gigantic scale, with accompanying social problems and areas of friction.

The Seine flows through the city in a wide arch, dividing her into two unequal halves, the *Rive Gauche* – the southern, "left" bank – and the *Rive Droite* – the northern, "right" bank. Two islands remain: the Ile de la Cité (home to Notre-Dame and Conciergerie) and the Ile St-Louis, one of the premier residential areas in the city.

The official "City of Paris," with a city prefect and a police prefect as the top elected officials, is split into 20 *arrondissements* (districts) and is further governed by a *Maire* (mayor) chosen by the Minister of the Interior. *La Défense*, a high-rise residential area, is considered the 21st *arrondissement*, even if it does not correspond geographically to the other arrondissements.

The division of the districts reflects the medieval organization of the city. The 1st, 2nd, and ninth arrondissements compose the "city," the important economic and government buildings. The 3rd, 4th, and 10th arrondissements involve mostly handcraft and private businesses. The 5th and parts of the 6th arrondissements house the university and publishing concerns, leading into the government, ministry, and diplomatic quarters of the western 6th and the 7th arrondissements. The 6th, 7th, 15th, and 16th arrondissements are the desirable, expensive residential areas. The remaining outer arrondissements are mostly mixed residential and business zones. The suburb ring consists of a collection of industrial complexes, residential blocks, commercial offices, and warehouses.

The Oppidum Lutetia (also known as Lucetia and Lucotecia) became a Roman colony in 51 B.C., existing for approximately 300 years with about 8.000 (primarily Celtic) settlers. The city began to grow, particularly on the slopes of the hill Ste-Geneviève to the south of the city. It was here, at the Rue Cujas, between the Boulevard St-Michel and the Rue St-Jacques, that the Forum was built, a structure perfectly suited to the carefully-designed street grid so typical of Roman colonies. The Cardo (the streets Rue St-Jacques and Rue St-Martin) was created to correspond with the original grand junction of streets; similarly, a Via Superior probably matched the Celtic trade route, while the new streets of Rue St-Michel and Rue St-Denis ran parallel to the Via Infe-

2.
Hotel de Ville, Paris, in
a painting from 1583.

3.
Nicolas J.B. Raguenet,
*Feast in Honour of the
Birth of the Duke of
Bourgogne*, 1751.

rior, and the Decumanus maximus (Rue Cujas - Rue Vaugirard) on the left bank found a mate in the Rue St-Antoine on the right bank. It is clear that the Roman government headquarters were on the Ile de la Cité, particularly the area on the western side of the island where the Palais de la Cité would later be built. Similarly, the cathedral of Notre-Dame was in all likelihood preceded by a temple.

The first evidence of Christianity in Paris dates back to the middle of the third century, largely on gravestones. According to the account of Gregor of Tours, St. Dionysius and his disciples were missionaries to the Galliens, although Dionysius was beheaded – legend holds at the foot of Montmartre – in 280 A.D. It is said that he was taken to his gravesite, Vicus Catulliacus, which would later become St-Denis, with his head in his hand. Probably around 300 A.D. Paris received its first bishop, whose cathedral may very well be buried beneath Notre-Dame.

Paris – which took this name during the reign of Julian Apostata around 360 A.D. – would come to play an important role in the defense of the Northwest Roman border against the invading Germans.

The Merovingians house, so named for Mérové (who leader between 448 and 458) ruled the core of what is now France until 751. The internal borders of the French territories changed rapidly between various primary regions – Austrasien, Neustrien, Burgundy – and various capital cities. In 508 Clovis I (reigned from 481 through 511) became the first ruler to elevate Paris to royal capital (from Soissons), after having slain the last Roman Duke in 486 and converted to Christianity.

With Pippin the Short's ascension in 751, Carolingian city government replaced the Merovingian. The city became rich through trade, and by 800 held around 20,000 to 30,000 inhabitants. With the election of Hugues Capet as Count of Paris and Duke of France, Paris finally became the royal capital. From this point until the revolution, the king was to decide upon the development and appearance of the city – even when he was living in Loire or in the fortresses and castles of the Ile-de-France. The royal influence on the city's character could be seen most overtly in the residences and the protective walls which now sprung up wherever development became more dense. By 1300, Paris had as many as 80,000 inhabitants (compared with around 40,000 for London).

Until the middle of the 13th century, Paris was the exclusive royal seat of a centralized state powerful enough to annex Anjou and Normandy in 1204 and Languedoc in 1229. Its citizens were

4.
Nicolas J.B. Raguenet,
Hotel de Ville, ca.
1750-1760.

"bourgeois du roi," existing sufficiently without the hallmarks of middle-class life common in the rest of Europe, standards like a city hall, a market plaza, and patrician palaces. These would not emerge until after 1350.

The 100 Years War sharply diminished the artistic life of the city. After the English imprisoned Jean le Bon in 1350-64 and Etienne Marcel led a revolt in 1356 against the monarchy, Charles V left his palace on the island for the more safe Louvre and the Hôtel St-Pol, protected by the Bastille, an imposing fortress on the Porte St-Antoine. He built new walls with protective ditches in the young northern districts and added more ditches to the city walls of Philippe Auguste the south. Over 1,400 aristocrats built their houses in the protected areas around the royal mansion in Marais and around the Louvre. The archbishop of Sens, under whose jurisdiction Paris fell until 1622, took shelter in the narrow Hôtel de Sens, and the abbot of Cluny took up at the fine Hôtel de Cluny.

Charles VII and Louis XII were the first to come in contact with the Italian Renaissance, although actual incorporation of Italian models waited until 1528 with the return of François I to Paris

13

from an Italian tour. He brought back the Italian master of the
Fontainebleau school to build his castle, which would set the architectural standard for a long time to come. The long religious
war which lasted until 1598 between the Catholic league and the
Protestant Huguenots limited artistic development severely,
however, and it was not until Henry IV, ruler between 1589-
1610 and the first of the Bourbons, switched to Catholicism that
architecture and fine arts regained prominence in France.

The Counter-Reformation and the Baroque era brought an important increase in new construction of religious buildings between 1610 and 1680, encouraged by the economic reforms and
increasingly peaceful climate fostered by Henry IV and his
minister Sully. Forty new cloisters and almost twenty new
churches were built in this era. There was also a corresponding
increase in secular buildings, including the extension of the Cour
Carrée of the Louvre by Louis XIII, Marie de Medici's Palais du
Luxembourg − designed like a provincial castle − Cardinal
Richelieu's mansion, and many Early Baroque town houses
like the Hôtel de Sully.

The Absolutism movement reached its apex during the reign of
Louis XIV (1643-1715), when the new "Grands Boulevards,"
magnificent wide streets running right up to the protective walls

5.
Pierre Antoine Machy,
*Laying the First Stone
for the Church of Ste-
Geneviève*, 1764.

6.
Pierre-Denise Martin,
*Louis XIV Entering
Paris, August 26th
1706, ca. 1710.*

of the city, flaunted the king's confidence against attack from
without or within.

It was not only churches and palaces that took up the push for
greater artistic and scientific heights – spurred by a king look-
ing for fame and glory – but also arenas of higher learning like
the Collège de France, manufacturing centers like the Gobelins,
and scientific institutions like the Observatory. Even social institutions like hospitals – i.e. the Hôpital St-Louis or the Hôtel
des Invalides – were first and foremost monuments to their financial patrons.

After the brief regency of Duke Philippe d'Orléans (1715-23),
Louis XV (1723-74) ushered in an artistic sensibility which largely followed the models of the 17th century. The Place Louis XV
was built as a royal plaza centered around a monument, on the
model of the Place de la Concorde. The Ecole Militaire on the
Champs de Mars, a tribute to the monarchy, followed the
form of the Hôtel des Invalides.

On another front, however, the Rococo movement explored fan-
tasy-inspired interior decoration of rooms themselves widely varied in form. The style moved to intimate apartments full of play-
fully asymmetric decorations which broke up the stiff grandeur
of the styles prevalent during Louis XIV's reign.

Soon thereafter, in the middle of the century, the strong, simplified forms of Neo-Classicism made their entrance, although some critics have expressed concerns that these were merely variations of the existing stylings of Louis XV. Major works in the years preceding the Revolution included the toll wall (Enceinte des Fermiers Généraux) built around Paris in 1785-86, and the many fantastically adorned gateways by the architect Ledoux.

The storming and razing of the Bastille on July 14, 1789 led to a tornado with the art world. Almost every Parisian church lost some of its decoration, and numerous churches were simply demolished. This confiscation of royal and church possession augured a radical reorganization of the city. Relying on plans drawn up by Edme Verniquet from 1773-91, the "Commission temporaire des artistes," a commission of architects, artists, and engineers, was formed in 1793 to make their recommendations for a new layout for Paris. Their suggestions included the rehabilitation of the old city and the continuation of the streets Rue de Rivoli, de Castiglione, and de la Paix.

The majority of the Revolutionary-style buildings were ephemeral, including triumph arches and altars built from wood, linen, and plaster for the celebrations on the Champs de Mars. Even during the First Republic (1792-1804), durable projects were rare. Bonapart's military Egyptian campaign of 1798 brought a taste for Egyptian decoration back to France, and Pompeian style similarly influenced many of the new buildings of that time.

Napoleon, who ruled in 1804-14, seized upon the municipal planning of the Revolutionary era. He extended the Rue de Rivoli to create an east-west axis. An arcade street trailed along the side wings of the Louvre, which themselves linked up with the Tuileries. The final vestiges of the medieval battlements – the Temple and Châtelet – gave way to plazas which let the traffic flow more smoothly. Napoleon himself favored the grandeur of ancient designs, arranging for the Madeleine to be built in the form of a temple and for a distinct temple façade to front the Palais Bourbon. Other projects continued in this vein, including the two triumph arches which proclaimed the glory of his victories: the magnificent and colorful Arc de Triomphe du Carrousel in the Louvre's courtyard and the gigantic Arc de Triomphe de l'Etoile, at the center of a wide radiating plaza. Interestingly, Paris's first iron structures also emerged under Napoleon: the Pont des Arts and the dome of the Halle du Blé/Bourse de Commerce. He also improved the municipal water and waste disposal situations, allowed streets to be built along the Seine, and paved countless others.

7.
Nicolas Edouard
Gabé, *Taking the
Pantheon*, 1848.
The Restoration (1814-48) put primary importance on repair-
ing Paris's buildings, particularly its churches. Quite a few re
ligious buildings were built after early Christian models, such
as St-Philippe-du-Roule, but no major projects appeared until the
St-Vincent-de-Paul church, where an early Christian pillared nave
was combined with a Grecian temple façade. A more typical project for the time were the expiatory chapels erected for the "martyrs" of the Revolution. Franz Christian Gau's basilica church Ste-
Clotilde-Ste-Valère was begun during this reign of Louis Philippe;
it would become the most important neo-Gothic building in the
city.

The issue of coping with the ever-increasing social and economic
problems moved to the forefront in the coming years. Migra-
tion from the countryside and industrialization ballooned the
city's population to around 1 million in 1850, and by 1870 it
was 2 million. A band of working-class suburbs sprung up
around the old city: St-Denis, Les Batignolles, and La Villette.
The unsatisfactory living and working conditions for the work-

ing masses led to even more riots and uprisings. Between 1841-45, a 36 kilometer protective wall, named for statesman Adolphe Thiers, fenced what is today the Boulevard Périphérique. This immediately added 7,800 hectares to the city's surface area. Through the addition of numerous train stations on the city's borders (St-Germain-en-Laye in 1837, St-Lazare in 1842, Gare de l'Est in 1835, Gare du Nord in 1857), city planners tried to alleviate the tremendous traffic congestion.

8.
Atget, Paris Cité Dorée, Boulevard de la Gare, 1912.

The first French civil planning ordinance was made law by the Second Republic (1848-52) in 1850. It called for the improvement of roads and of the unhygienic living conditions through such measures as the expropriation of private property. Napoleon III seized upon this during his second reign (1852-70), ordering his prefect, Georges E. Haussmann, to execute an unprecedented reorganization of the city. The slums of the city (Ile de la Cité) were broken up through the placement of important new buildings like the Supreme Court, hospitals, and barracks in their centers; streets along the Seine were cut into two; large boulevards like Sébastopol, St-Michel, and St-Germain were laid in a grid through the old city; and the main train stations were linked through a beltway. Parks and gardens were built in the inner city, including the Square de la Tour St-Jacques from 1854, the Bois de Vincennes in the east, the northern Parc des Buttes-Chaumont, the Bois de Boulogne to the west, and the Parc des Montsouris to the south.

At the same time, numerous historical buildings were renovated and excavated by Jean-Baptiste Antoine Lassus and Eugène Viollet-le-Duc. Many of these became key destinations on the many new streets, although they were often forced to conform with new construction regulations demanded that buildings be either 5 or 6 stories high and include continuous balconies with metal gratings. Even if Haussmann and his colleagues destroyed many buildings which might have been considered artistic, they saved the city from implosion. The effects of those ordinances can still be seen today on many streets in the uniformity of building heights and façade design. In any case, the mixing of classes, with rich and poor living in close proximity, often separated only by floors, produced results more socially acceptable than other municipal theories.

The Second Empire ended with the German-French War of 1870-71, when a siege on the city and a tremendous misery among the workers led to a revolt against the Republic. With the rebuilding of City Hall, the Third Republic created a grandiose monument for itself. Even as the ruins of the Tuileries were

cleaned up and the noble Louvre was reopened, this center of the bourgeois government seemed like a giant Loire castle, with its prefect living in royal salons. The Roman-Byzantine pilgrim's church Sacré-Cœur, built as a *Vœu national* in 1870-75, was meant to help France heal from the wounds caused by the violent Commune uprising.

In the second half of the 19th century, the focus moved away from the gigantic public buildings, which contented themselves with the styles of the previous century. Instead, creative iron and iron-and-glass architecture emerged in Victor Baltard's Halles, which were both a marvel of engineering and an important center for health care. Numerous glass corridors were constructed in the shopping districts for luxury items, and gigantic stores were created for the masses (Au Bon Marché, among others). Impressive iron structures like the Palais de l'Industrie and the Galerie des Machines were built for the World's Fair, which Paris hosted in 1855, 1867, 1878, 1889, and 1900. The Eiffel Tower, extremely controversial during its construction, was built for the 1889 World's Fair, where it became a symbol of the city's progressiveness. The 1900 World's Fair left behind two exhibit halls with ashlar façades, the Grand and the Petit Palais, as well as the neo-Baroque Pont Alexandre III and the magnificent Gare d'Orsay train station (1898-1900) by Victor Laloux. Two churches built in the last years of the century created a stir: St-Jean-l'Evangéliste, a cement and iron building by Anatole de Baudot, and the Notre-Dame-du-Travail, built by Jules Astruc of rolled iron.

The Art Nouveau movement around the turn of the century replaced the designs of the 19th century with organic ornamentation and found its most pure expression in buildings by the designer Hector Guimard.

As successful as the inventive decorator Guimard's buildings were the iron-and-concrete works of August Perret; the First were more modern and influential, inspiring builders like François Hennebique to create masterpieces like his house on the Rue Danton. Perret's buildings – the garage on the Rue Ponthieu and the Théâtre des Champs-Elysées, among many others – awed and inspired onlookers through their great economy of material and effort, as well as their tremendous potential for standardization and industrialization of concrete construction.

Even though numerous buildings from the post-War era deserve mention, few coherent threads of development run through that era. In 1949-51, Jean Prouvé built the first curtained façade, for the Fédération Nationale Bâtiment. The CNIT (Centre National des Industries et Techniques) exhibition hall at La Défense set the standard in 1956 for concrete vaulting. Beginning in 1964, the high-rise apartments of the "21st" arrondissement were built, with interesting variations from their American models.

Irrepressibly individualistic are Henri Bernard's ring-shaped Maison de Radio-France (1952-63), the Y-shaped headquarters of UNESCO (build in 1955-58 by Marcel Breuer, among others), the round Palais des Sports (1959 by Pierre Dufau and others), and the curved, rectangular glass offices of the French Communist Party (1965-71 by Oscar Niemeyer and others.) Around 1970, the unquestionable masterpiece was Roger Taillibert's Parc-des-Princes Stadium, resembling a huge concrete sculpture.

The 1970s brought few uplifting projects: the Forum des Halles (begun 1973), a glassy crater; the Australian Embassy (1978), an antiquated concrete structure; the Totem Tower (1978), with clusters apartment cubicles within a concrete frame. Even less inspiring were the 15 high-rises of the "Front de Seine."

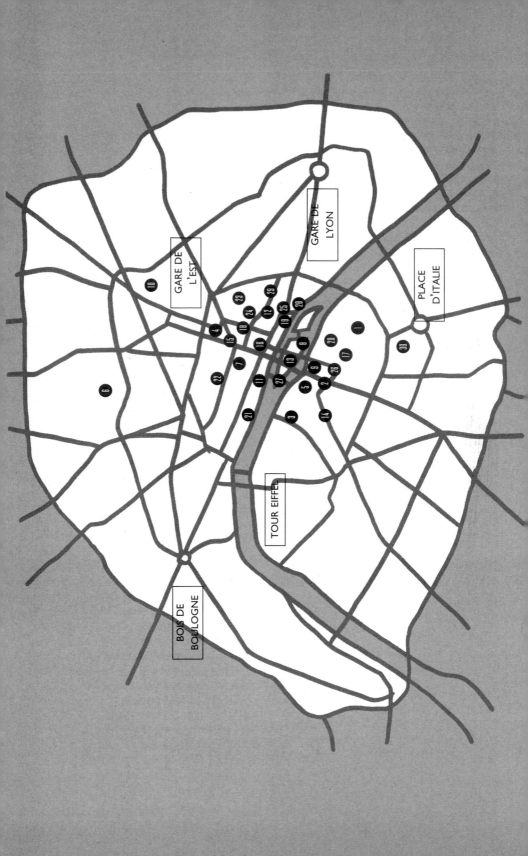

The Beginnings of Paris

Only a few hints of architecture have survived from the early Roman settlement Oppidum Lutetia. Extensive excavations have brought to life the monumental, 160×100 meter Forum. Important above-ground remains of thermal baths can be seen in the Museé de Cluny, while subterranean structures are found beneath the Collège de France. The remains of a 15-meter-long aqueduct can be seen at Arcueil. A large (130×100 meter) 2nd century amphitheater has been unearthed and partially reconstructed, and a small theater lies beneath the Lycée St-Louis. Under King Clovis (481-511), Paris became capital of the Frankish kingdom. His conversion to Christianity in 496 paralleled the larger French conversion to that religion and precipitated the founding of a circle of cloisters around the city: to the north, St-Gervais-St-Protais, St-Germain-l'Auxerrois, St-Laurent and St-Martin-des-Champs; to the south St-Germain-des-Prés, Ste-Geneviève, St-Médard, St-Marcel and St-Victor. Each of these branches brought a small settlement with them, first called bourg and later faubourg. Capetian Hugues Capet (987-996) elevated Paris for the first time to the royal seat and hence the center of the French kingdom. The 10th century saw a colony of traders and craftsmen on the right bank of the Seine, and the university developed in the 12th century. Philippe II Auguste united these three city districts between 1190 and 1220 by building a city wall. In 1183 he allowed the first market, Les Halles, to be set up and then broke ground in 1200 for the stronghold which preceded the Louvre. Around 1163, Bishop Maurice de Sully broke ground on Notre-Dame, which was to be the paragon of Early Gothic religious architecture. The reign of Louis IX (1226-70), known as the Holy One, saw the construction of Sainte-Chapelle.

1

Lutetian Arena
ca. 100 B.C.
49, Rue Monge, 5e
Metro: Monge

This oval, Roman-style theater, first built around 100 B.C., was unearthed during road construction in 1869. Its theater (100×130 meters) could be utilized as both an amphitheater for an audience of 15,000 and a dramatic space, with a 41-meter stage along the valley and viewing galleries on the cliffs of Mons Luticius. The entire space was restored and expanded in 1915-18 by Louis J. Capitan.

2

Cluny Baths
ca. 200 B.C.
6, Place Paul-Painlevé, 5e
Metro: Maubert-Mutualité

Most of the important ruins from these Roman thermal baths, the largest in Paris around 200 B.C., can be viewed above ground. It was built from brick and ashlar slabs, with groin vaulting atop drums in the *frigidarium* (cold baths). Atop the four remaining consoles are relief works depicting a ship's prow, weapons, and tritons, probably the trademarks of boatmen from the Seine employed in the construction of the baths. Note the further vaulted substructures (10×65 meters) by the downward-sloped land-ing, as well as the main façade whose two symmetric halls face north. The baths, renamed "Palais des Thermes" in 1138, were rediscovered in 1829, annexed to the Musée de Cluny in 1843, and eventually excavated between 1947 and 1957.

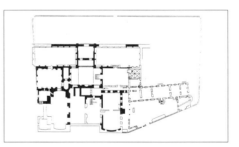

3

St-Germain-des-Prés
11th-12th century
Place St-Germain-des-Prés, 6e

Metro: St-Germain-des-Prés

According to legend, Childebert the First brought the tunic of St. Vincentius and a golden cross from Saragossa to Paris in 542. To house these relics, he built this church and cloister, which were to become the gravesite of the Merovingian kings. These initial buildings were consecrated in 558 by Bishop Germanus (d. 576), named the patron saint of the church after his canonization in 754. That triple-transept church, whose marbled column shafts now grace the triforium of the main church, made way during the reign of Abbey Morardus (990-1014) to early Roman style re-

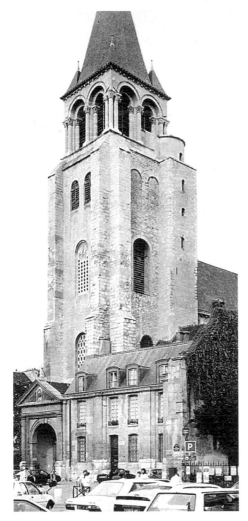

building, still visible in the sturdy, unadorned western tower, hand hewn from ashlar slabs. Ribbed vaults dating back to 1644-46 enclose the 65-meter long nave (mid-11th century), which features 5 bays and three transepts, the middle of which is a full 7 meters wide and 9 meters high. The bay design, the arching patterns, and the elevation created by rounded arcades all belong to an approach to stone work which is echoed in the middle transept and in the three-part choir with flanking towers over the front bays of the fore-apse. The excessively gilded column capitals are noteworthy for their figure ornamentation, although many of the capitals have been replaced (twelve originals can be found in the Musée de Cluny). The Early Gothic choir with a gallery and five radiating chapels (including an arcade above rounded pillars, fine acanthus capitals with animal decorations, a triforium as double arcade under pointed blind arches, and rounded arched windows) is an offshoot of the Early Gothic cathedrals of the Ile-de-France (Nyon, for example). It was begun in 1150 and consecrated by Pope Alexander III in 1163, the same year ground was broken on the Notre-Dame cathedral. A symbolic western portal was also created at this time, although only the lintel (inscribed with the phrase "evening bread") remains. The foyer was added in 1608-09. The ruins of a High Gothic cloister, built by architect Pierre de Mountreuil from 1239-44 to enliven the refectory but destroyed in 1802, can be seen on the nearby Square Laurent-Prace.

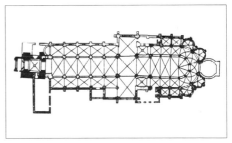

4

St-Martin-des-Champs
12th century
292, Rue St-Martin, 3e

Metro: Arts et Métiers

This cloister, built in 1060 for Henry I on the site of an old shrine to St. Martin, was, at the time, the largest such structure in the immediate vicinity of the city. It was entrusted in 1079 to the Cluny abbey, and endured Prior Hugo I's addition of a walled priory from 1130-42 (ruins still visible). Hugo I also oversaw the construction of the polygonal, Late Roman-Early Gothic choir with dual galleries, and circular and keystone chapels, all of which influenced Suger's famous choir in the St-Denis cathedral. Particularly noteworthy are the spatial asymmetries, including the floor and ceiling heights, and the distances between each buttress, arch and vault. The nave and its wooden ceiling date back to the middle of the 13th century, although both were restored in the 19th century. The façades were renovated in 1764 and 1885. The refectory (1235), a small, high room of Gothic design with ribbed vaults on rounded pillars and clustered windows, now acts as the reading room of the museum's library. After the dissolution of the cloister in 1791, the building was occupied by the National Conservatory for the Arts (founded 1794) in 1798.

5

St-Séverin
13th century
1, Rue des Prêtres-St-Séverin, 5e

Metro: Maubert-Mutualité

This church is rumored to have been built on the grave of the early settler Severin (d. 565). Many sections of this basilica with dual, polygonal choir galleries (5 naves, 8 bays, 58×38×17 meters) date back to a 13th century church, including the foundations of the towers, the western bay and the innermost nave on the southern side. The second southern side nave was added around 1350. The remaining sections were rebuilt after a fire in 1448. Note the multi-part star vaulting in the choir passage – the rest of the church is cross vaulted.

26

6

St-Pierre-de-Montmartre
12th century
2, Rue du Mont-Cenis, 18e
Metro: Abbesses

The modest exterior of this Roman parish church belies its historical importance: this northern hill of Paris is named in remembrance of the beheading of St. Dionysius and his companions in

272. (Montmarte means "Mountain of the Martyr.") It also housed a Roman temple to Mercury and later a 7th century church which, after being destroyed several times, became a Benedictine nunnery in 1134. At the time of its consecration, only the easternmost section of the modern church had been completed, with 3 apses, towers over the bays of the antechoir, a transept, and a bay on the eastern side of the nave. The torus moldings on middle bay of the front choir resemble those in the western wing of the St-Denis church, making them the oldest in Paris. The remainder of the nave, with three transepts, 3 more bays, and a three-part elevation resembling a triforium around the roof-truss, was completed in the middle of the 12th century, although the main apse was replaced around the turn of that century for one of Early Gothic design and the façades were replaced in 1775. The cloister was moved in 1686, including the removal of some sections of the building. The site was extensively (perhaps excessively) restored from 1834-74 and from 1899-1905, with a new excavation in 1976-78.

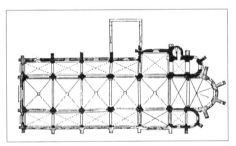

7

St-Leu-St-Gilles
after 1319
92bis, Rue St-Denis, 1er
Metro: Etienne Marcel

This church, dedicated to both a rustic hermit and a bishop from Sens, was purposefully hemmed in to accommodate the houses on the Boulevard de Sébastopol. Construction began in 1235; the pillared portal harks from that time. A low-lying one room church was constructed in 1319, which has been incorporated as the 6-bay nave. Side naves were added during 16th century expansion, as were the high choir with a gallery and the Late Gothic circular chapel. In 1860 a neo-Renaissance eastern end was added by Victor Baltard.

8

Notre-Dame Cathedral
after 1163
Place du Parvis-Notre Dame, 4e
Metro: Cité

This 130-meter long cathedral for Bishop Maurice de Sully (1160-96) was begun in 1163 and culminated in a long string of buildings on this site. A Gaulish-Roman shrine was replaced in the 6th century by a family of churches which had been destroyed during the Norman invasion at the end of the 11th century and subsequently rebuilt. Its foundations lay beneath and in front of the façade of the current cathedral, with a baptismal font to the north and a church consecrated to Notre Dame to the east, under the modern choir. The modern cathedral exhibits model Early Gothic form, with five naves, a uniform façade for the dual towers, a medium-sized transept, a long choir with twin galleries, a row of chapels, a four-story elevation (comprised of rounded-pillar arcades, vaulted ceilings, a round triforium, screened windows, and a six-part ribbed vault) with direct proportioning. It was constructed in 7 stages:

I. The area from the choir to the eastern wall of the transept was constructed 1163-82. The main altar was consecrated in 1182.
II. The three eastern bays of the nave were built from 1180-1200.
III. From 1200-25, the foundation for the tower and the western bays of the nave were laid with segmented, rounded pillars. The area utilized a three portal construction with rich sculptural adornment. To the left is a Marian Portal, with a Marian crown atop its tympanum, and reliefs on its column shafts and on the door frame. The figures on its frame have been restored. The middle work is the Portal of Justice, whose door supports and middle columns were removed in 1771 and which has reliefs of the virtues and sins on its frame. To the right is Anne's Portal, finished ca. 1160. The Gallery of kings, believed to have housed the remains of 28 kings, was destroyed in 1793.
IV. Towers were constructed from 1225-50.
V. Rebuilding of the upper reaches, with the installation of huge tracery windows to better the interior lighting, and reconfiguration of the buttress system (one arch instead of two). The original four-story high elevation was returned to the crossing only in the 19th century.
VI. A new transept was built in the north from 1246-47 with a statue of Mary and two figure supports. The southern façade of the nave was completed by Jean de Chelles and his disciple Pierre de Mountreuil in 1258.
VII. 1296-1330 saw construction of the choir chapels in the apses, the high windows of the choir and a revision of the choir buttresses.

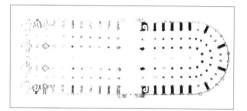

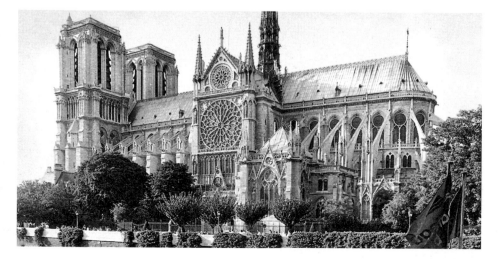

9

St-Julien-le-Pauvre
after 1165-70
1, Rue St-Julien-le-Pauvre, 5e
Metro: St-Michel

This small building, tucked between trees and old houses, measures but 21.8 meters in length and belongs to a group of six Merovingian churches that were christened by St. Gregor of Tours in 582. Its name honors the martyr Julian of Brioude (d. ca. 300 A.D.) as well the bishop Julian (d. 1st century) of Le Mans. The smallish cloister offered a hospice at the crossroads of several important Roman roads, although it had been a Benedictine priory of the Longpont abbey since 1120. The triple-aisle, Early Gothic basilica form takes after the Notre Dame cathedral, with three semicircular, decidedly Roman apses, a choir with twin bays, alternating pillars and ceiling ribs, in 6 parts, on capitals with symbols of "service," "trees," and "budding" including the famous Harpy capital. In 1651, the early 13th-century nave lost the two westernmost of its six bays, its façade, and its triforium; the ribbing was also transformed into a barrel vault. After 1653, it was used as the chapel for the Hôtel-Dieu until its closure in 1793. Since 1889, it has served as a Greek Orthodox (Melchitian) shrine.

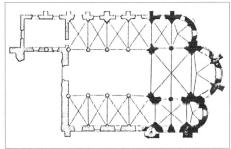

10

St-Laurent
ca. 1400
68, Boulevard de Strasbourg, 10e
Metro: Gare de l'Est

As early as 583 there was mention of a Laurentian chapel by St. Gregor of Tours, although a parish church has existed on this site since at least 1180, with the tower as a remnant of those early days. The polygonal choir gallery was begun in 1400 and consecrated 29 years later. The simple nave and five side aisles were begun in 1500, yet were only slowly completed. Antoine Lepautre's Baroque gabled façade of 1621 was later replaced with a neo-Gothic front from 1863-67. The vaulting was constructed from 1655-59.

11

St-Germain-l'Auxerrois
12th–15th century
2, Place du Louvre, 1er
Metro: Pont Neuf

The tower foundations (to the south of the current choir) of this five-aisle parish church were begun in the 12th century, and it was dedicated to the bishop of Auxerre (d. 448). After protective city walls were installed in the district by Philippe II Auguste, the church was safely occupied around 1200 A.D., with its Portal of Justice built between 1220-30. The choir and inner corridor were built in the 13th century along with the southernmost aisle and the Virgin's chapel. The nave and the remaining aisles were renovated from 1420-25, and Jean Caussel's richly decorated "burgundy" portico was constructed simultaneously with the transept and the northern side chapel (1435-39). A second choir corridor and chapel were built from 1500-30, and in 1754 the women's choir was reconfigured, including the removal of the Pierre Lescot and Jean Goujon's choir screen (remnants are stored in the Louvre). Baron

Haussmann performed major renovations on the church, including lengthening it to the north.

12

Temple des Billettes
completed 1427
24, Rue des Archives, 4e
Metro: Hôtel de Ville

Built in 1294 to honor of Communion as an expiatory chapel, this church was given over to the workers of the Billettes hospital of the Charité Notre-Dame by Philippe le Bel in 1299. Notice the cumbersome late-Gothic pillared crossing (completed in 1427), the last of its kind in Paris. From 1755-58 the Dominican monk Claude, added a barrel vault and Ionic pillars over the nave and rib vaulted side aisles, with a gallery and an almost circular choir. Since 1812 it has served as a Lutheran church.

13
Sainte-Chapelle
1246-48
4, Boulevard du Palais, 1er
Metro: Cité

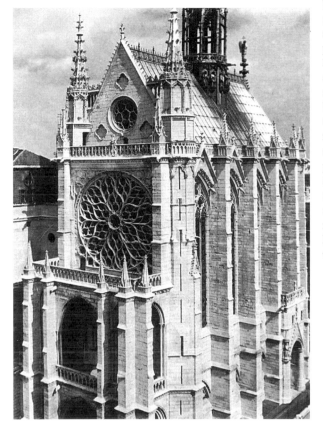

Located in the courtyard of the Supreme Court, this High Gothic palace chapel of St. Louis is the oldest wing of this medieval manor. After Louis IX acquired the Crown of Thorns and several other Passion relics from Byzantium in 1239, he built this enormous chapel (36×17× 43.5 meters) as their shrine. The chief architect was probably a student of Robert de Luzarches of Amiens. It features a two-story, ribbed vault construction, with a western portico beneath the tabernacle, a low, three-aisle ground floor for the members of the court, and a slender, non-weight bearing upper floor for the royal family and the relics, ending in stained tracery windows. The chapel also sports a polygonal choir. The remains of the relics elevation lie in the apse. The western rose window was restored in 1485.

14
Couvent des Cordeliers
15th century
15, Rue de l'Ecole-de-Médecine, 6e
Metro: Odéon

In 1230, the abbey Euides from St-Germain-des-Prés gave over land for the construction of a cloister of Franciscan monks (the Cordeliers order, named after their belts). Although these mendicants, supported by the court, constructed extensive structures including a transept church – only the large, dual aisle, 4-bayed refectory (56×17 meters, wood supports) remains. The refectory itself was built only at the end of the 15th century with financial support from Anne de Bretagne.

15

St-Nicolas-des-Champs

1420-80
254, Rue St-Martin, 3e

Metro: Réaumur-Sébastopol

The first mention of a chapel at this site was in 1119, but it is clear that a parish church was in place here by 1184. A modest late-Gothic structure was erected from 1420-80, with a façade (figures renovated in 1843) with three gables, a tower to the southern side, 6 bays off the western side of the basilica nave, and the original side aisle to the south. Further construction around 1541 added a second neo-Renaissance side aisle. The nave was lengthened to the east through 4 more bays (1567-87). The remaining outer side aisles, chapels, and the notable southern portal (dated 1581, from designs by Philibert de l'Orme; the door panel dates from the same period). The remaining two choir bays, the double choir galleries (netted vaulting), and the chapel circle were added from 1613-15. The pillars in the choir were converted in 1745 to fluted Doric columns.

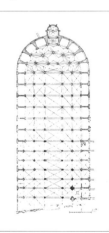

16

St-Jacques Tower

1508-22
Jean de Félin
Square de la Tour St-Jacques, 4e

Metro: Châtelet

The tracery-decorated tower from Jean de Félin (1508-22) is the sole remains of the Late Gothic Jacobean church (destroyed 1797), which had been entrusted since 1259 to the fisherman's guild. The tower was restored in 1853 and its figures completed.

17

St-Etienne-du-Mont

after 1492
Etienne Viguier
1, Place Ste-Geneviève, 5e

Metro: Luxembourg-Cardinal Lemoine

Until 1807, this parish church, a baffling mix of flamboyant Gothic and Renaissance style, stood directly to the north of the Ste-Geneviève abbey, to which it belonged. The original structure was built around 1221; the current building is modeled on the Notre-Dame cathedral and

stretches at its middle to 68×29×23.5 meters, with a modest Late Gothic choir gallery and chapel circle (built in 1492 under the leadership of Viguier). The eastern section was completed up to the transept in 1539, including star vaulting with a drooping keystone in the crossing. The wicker choir-screens, a decorative masterpiece of the French Renaissance, date back at least as far as 1541 and 1545, when they were mentioned in correspondence to Antoine Beaucorps. The portico dates to 1605, from Pierre Biard. The broad, hall-like nave dates to 1580; notice the curious walkway which circles halfway up the rounded pillars. The characteristic shrine façade by Claude Guérin was completed from 1610-22. Final consecration came in 1626.

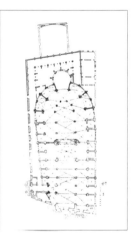

18

St-Merri

ca. 1515
78, Rue St-Martin, 4e

Metro: Hôtel de Ville

A Late Gothic parish church with a 70-meter long, multi-aisle basilica with transept, extended choir, gallery, and circular chapel was built atop the site of the chapel in which the abbot Merri was interred around 700 A.D. The ground plan is a reduced take-off of the Notre-Dame cathedral, which St-Merri joined as a chapter in 1005. The church was completed in stages, with the nave finished in 1520. The transept followed in 1526, and the choir (polygonal, with a rectangular chapel) was finished in 1552.

19

St-Gervais-St-Protais
1494-1657
2, Rue François-Miron, 4e

Metro: St-Paul

This is perhaps the oldest parish church on the right bank, although only the tower foundation remains from the original Gothic church (begun in 1220, consecrated in 1420) that was dedicated to two martyrs. Its successor, a 76-meter, two-story pillared basilica church with three naves and a circular choir with gallery, was built between 1494 and 1657, allegedly by plans from Martin Chambiges. The choir was completed in 1540, the Renaissance transept arm in 1578, and the star-vaulted nave (part of a steep, two-story Gothic structure) in the years 1600-20. Louis XIII began construction of the façade in 1616, his support won through the combined efforts of Salomon de Brosse and Clément II Métezeau: it was completed as a monumental three-story picture wall with intertwining doubled columns beneath a segmented, arched gable.

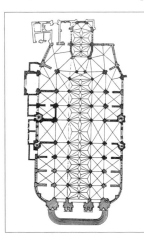

20

City walls of Philippe Auguste
after 1190
4th and 5th (including Rue des Jardins St-Paul, Rue Clovis and Rue des Fossés St-Jacques)

Metro: Pont Marie, Luxembourg

Two large pieces of the city walls are still visible, built by King Philippe Auguste around 1190 to secure that half of the city. One sits on the Rue des Jardins St-Paul, the other on the Rue Clovis (here numbers 3-7, 200 meters long and over 10 meters high.)

21

Palais du Louvre
Place du Louvre, 1er

Metro: Palais-Royal

The somewhat complicated story of this complex, the former French royal palace and currently one of the largest museums in the world, can be condensed into eight primary phases:

I. The medieval castle emerged around 1190-1200 under Philippe II Auguste as a river stronghold, with four wings cornered by rounded towers protecting a round donjon. On the orders of Charles V it was converted in 1370 into a palace. The royal residence, however, remained at the Palais de la Cité and the Hôtel St-Pol.

II. The donjon was demolished in 1527 and in 1516 a Renaissance construction was planned by Pierre Lescot for François I, eventually completed under the reign of Henry II. It featured a three-story corps de logis in the western section of the Cour Carrée, three forepart, reliefs on the pilasters, half columns and niches, as well as figural adornment by Jean Goujon and his workshop.

III. 1564 brought the construction of the Tuileries palace by Philibert de l'Orme for Catherine de' Medici, as well as plans to link the two state castles. The Petite Galerie was built down to the river in 1566, probably by Lescot, and a Grande Galerie was extended along the river by Henry IV from 1595 to 1608.

IV. Under Louis XIII, the Cour Carrée was constructed by Jacques Lemercier, who quadrupled Lescot's planned measurements and installed high pavilions in the middle of the long wings

V. The Petite Galerie was improved and extended by Louis Le Vau,

VI. Le Vau completed the Cour Carrée between 1659-74. The combined efforts of Le Vau, Lebrun and Perrault (with influences by Bernini's design plans) led to the 1667-70 construction of the 183-meter long eastern façade, the most famous of the Louvre's colonnades and the first major work of the Baroque-Classical movement. The artwork was installed in 1674, and in 1678 the royal residence shifted to Versailles. The Louvre was soon divided into artist's studios and academies.

VII. The castle became a "Musée de la République" in 1793, later renamed the "Musée Napoléon" in 1803. Napoleon's reign also saw the revisiting of plans to link the Louvre and the Tuileries, and from 1806-12 a wing was built on Rue de Rivoli by Charles Percier and Pierre-François-Léonard Fontaine.

VIII. From 1852-82, during his second reign, Napoleon III finally had Louis T.J. Visconti connect the Tuileries and Louvre and build the symmetric neo-Baroque side wings in the second courtyard. Hector M. Lefuel completed this work.

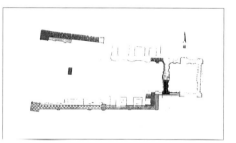

22

Tower of Jean sans Peur
14th century
20, Rue Etienne-Marcel, 2e
Metro: Etienne Marcel

The sole remains of the extensive Hôtel de Bourgogne is the defensive tower from the beginning of the 14th century, which is today part of a school. It was square in shape, with windows and loopholes, a spiral staircase, and branched vaulting. The coat-of-arms of Duke Jean sans Peur of Burgundy can be seen above the arch.

23

Hôtel de Clisson
after 1380
58, Rue des Archives, 3e
Metro: Rambuteau, Bus 75

This squared gate with rounded towers and a pointed arched portal is the last remains of a late medieval city mansion built for Olivier de Clisson, constable of France beginning in 1380. The coat-of-arms signify the Duke of Guide, who owned the estate in 1553. Although the decorations by Nicolò dell'Abate have disappeared, the chapel remains. The construction of the Hôtel de Soubise (begun 1700) signaled the downfall of this important mansion; on the site of the original keep is the "Salon ovale" by Germain Boffrand.

24

Maison de Nicolas Flamel
1407
Nicolas Flamel
51, Rue de Montmorency, 3e
Metro: Rambuteau

This house, one of the oldest in all of Paris, was built by the university secretary Nicolas Flamel (d. 1418) as a homeless shelter with the name "Le Grand Pignon." The four stories are built of robust ashlar; the ground floor features three entrances and two windows, with three floors for residents above. The long inscription on the cornice instructs those who are accepted within to pray in memory of the dead. The house was restored between 1900 and 1909.

25

Maison "a l'enseigne du faucheur" and Maison "a l'enseigne du mouton"
14th–15th century
11–13, Rue François-Miron, 4e
Metro: St-Paul

These two late medieval half-timbered houses, both probably dating from the 14th or 15th centuries, are close in proximity and design, with two axes and businesses on their ground floors levels. The two buildings were restored in 1967.

26

Hôtel de Cluny
ca. 1500
6, Place Paul-Painlevé, 5e
Metro: Odéon

This residence, along with the Hôtel de Sens, is perhaps the masterpiece of secular Late Gothic Parisian architecture. Pierre de Chatellux, abbot of Cluny (a Burgundy cloister), took possession of this former Roman thermal site in 1330 with the intent of building a college. Instead, abbot Jacques d'Amboise (1485-1510) built the current structure, with its merloned walls, irregular courtyard with a fountain, three asymmetric wings with horizontal cornices, cross windows, buttressed balustrades, spiral staircases, and rich adornment like coats of arms and Jacobean emblems. Note the squared space with a beam ceiling and fireplaces, the magnificent house chapel, the square room with fan vaulting over thin columns, (with twelve kneeling figures of the abbot in the baldachins and in the vaulting of the apses windows–depicting the Holy Father, the Crucifixion, and the Angel with Passion relics). It was restored from 1843-44 by Albert Lenoir and has been a part of the Musée de Cluny since 1844.

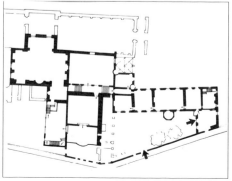

27

Conciergerie and Palais de Justice
ca. 1300
Quai de l'Horloge, 1er

Metro: Cité

This medieval residence of the French rulers was built on the western point of the Seine island on the lands of the Merovingian kings and the Count of Paris (House of Capetinger, crowned king in 987), over Roman battlements and 4th century palaces.

The oldest ruins, extensively renovated, hail from the age of Philippe le Bel, for whom they were built from 1296-1313 by Enguerrand de Marginy. Up until the construction of streets along the banks in 1611, the four towers of the façade ran directly along the water. The Tour de l'Horloge (built 1350, clock added around 1370 under Henry III, decorated in 1583 by G. Pilon) is flanked by three rounded 14th century watch towers. Several vaulted halls stood on the ground floor behind this row of towers, including the twin-aisle "Salle des Gardes" (23×12 meters, built at the end of the 14th century), the "Salle des Gens d'Armes" (1300-10, with 4 aisles, 9 bays, measuring 70×30 meters and 8 meters high), and the "Cuisines des St-Louis," a square room with four corner fireplaces, built from 1350-53. Beneath these rib vaulted spaces lay the dungeon and prison for revolutionaries.

Charles V gave the palace up in 1358 in favor of the Hôtel St-Pol in Marais and left the concierge to administer it. Charles VII transferred its control to the parliament in 1431. The most important parts of the courthouse, which encompasses several courtyards, were built after conflagrations in 1618, 1737, and 1776. Three wings were added to the Cour du Mai by Jacques D. Antoine from 1783-86, with the magnificent railings courtesy of Thomas Bigonnet. The structure was extended through longer columned façades to the Rue de Harlay between 1857-68 by Joseph L. Duc and Honoré Daumet. A wing was added from 1911-14 to the Quai des Orfèvres by Albert Tournaire.

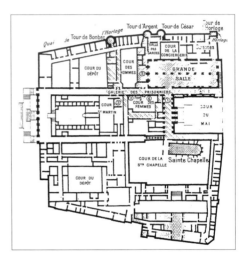

38

28
Hôtel de Sens
1474-1519
1, Rue du Figuier, 4e
Metro: Pont Marie

This Late Gothic building served as the residence of Tristan de Salazar, the archbishop of Sens. The spacious, multiple-winged structure surrounds an irregular courtyard, with three ashlar floors with horizontal cornices, cross windows, richly decorated skylights, and small round towers bordering the fortified entrances. Renovations have been of mixed quality. It has been in the possession of the city since 1911, and has housed the Bibliothèque Forney since 1961. Its gorgeous Renaissance garden borders the Rue de Fourcy.

29
Hôtel Hérouet
after 1499
Jean Malingre
57, Rue Vieille-du-Temple, 3e
Metro: St-Paul

This small, Late Gothic corner house with fantastic cross windows was built by Malingre, an advisor of the king, at the turn of the 16th century. It was severely damaged by the bombarding of 1944, but everything except the square tower (bracket-supported, with buttressed relief) has been restored.

30
Hôtel de la Reine Blanche
beginning of 16th century
17, Rue des Gobelins
Metro: Gobelins

The Gobelins probably owned this solid, rectangular structure, graced with polygonal towers with spiral staircases on its corners, a flat half-timber gallery over a flat arched gate, and a steep roof. Restorations are planned.

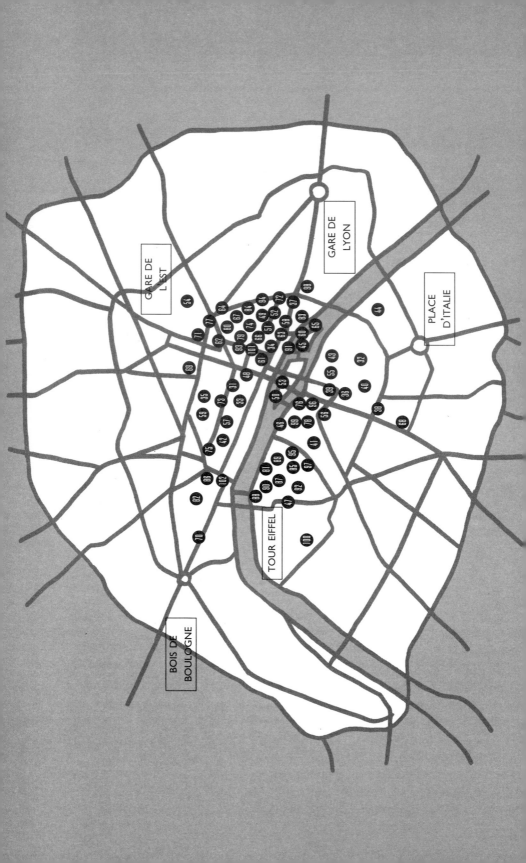

Sacred and Secular Buildings from the Renaissance through Rococo

François I's (1515-47) return from his Italian visit signaled a new era of French acquisition and integration of Italian Renaissance models. Pierre Lescot began his "new" Louvre in 1546 following these models. St-Eustache, which after 1532 competed with Notre-Dame for the title of France's largest Renaissance church, took on the purity of Italian decoration in a Gothic style.

Henry IV, first of the Bourbons, and his vision of city design – planning instead of wild growth, precise axes, symmetric plazas, standardized houses and neighborhoods – engendered the Place Royale-Place des Vosges and the Place Dauphine with the Pont Neuf, the beginnings of modern city planning in France. The Counterreformation and the Baroque era brought an important chain of new religious buildings between 1610 and 1680. During those decades, 40 new cloisters were founded in Paris and almost 20 new churches were built. St. Paul's and St. Louis', two marvelous Jesuit churches, were followed by an important series of Roman-inspired domed buildings that altered the city's skyline: Richelieu's burial church, Ste-Ursule-de-la-Sorbonne (begun in 1635 by Jacques Lemercier); the Benedictine Val-de-Grâce church (begun in 1645 by François Mansart) for Queen Anne D'Autriche; Mazarin's burial church in the Collège des Quatre-Nations (begun in 1661 by Louis Le Vau) and the Invalid church; and the burial church of the Sun King, actually just a monumental dome with a base.

1665 saw the emergence of a new trend in Parisian city planning: the construction of the inner ring of Grands Boulevards with triumph arches in the place of the old protection walls. Beginning in 1681, monumental plazas like the Place Victoires and Place Vendôme were situated in the aristocratic quarters.

41

31

St-Eustache
1532-1640
2, Rue du Jour, 1er

Metro: Les Halles

The original market hall was built near this spot in 1183 under Philippe II Auguste, and in 1213 an Agnes chapel was built for the merchants here. Paris's first Renaissance building was erected here under François I in 1532: an artistic, free-standing, five-aisle basilica church with a transept, two galleries, chapel aisles, a divided chapel, and four-part ribbed vaulting. It was built in 6 stages (architect unknown), and finally finished in 1640. The oldest part is the transept, followed by the steep nave. The choir was built later (1623-37) on the spot of the old church. The floor plan, buttressing, and general structure borrow overtly from the Notre-Dame cathedral, although the Renaissance forms emerge strongly in the non-traditional approach taken for the supports.

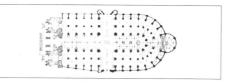

32

St-Médard
16th century
141, Rue Mouffetard, 5e

Metro: Censier-Daubenton

As early as 1163 there was mention of a small church, fully dependent on the abbey of Ste-Geneviève, located within the hollow of the Bièvre (a small, canaled river) which had been consecrated by the Bishop of Noyon (d. 545). A Late Gothic nave (three aisles, ribbed vaulting) from the middle or second half of the 16th century was followed by a light Late Renaissance choir with a gallery and chapel (1550-86 and 1609-22). A Marian chapel was added in 1784, and the choir pillars were converted into Doric columns by Louis F. Petit-Radel.

33

Oratoire du Louvre (Temple de l'Oratoire)
1621-30
Jacques Lemercier
145, Rue St-Honoré, 1er
Metro: Palais-Royal

In 1611, Pierre de Bérulle founded the French branch of the Oratorianer, whose church was built here through support of the Métezeau family (plans by Lemercier). The result is a proportioned chamber nicely with a gallery above the rectangular chapel. Note the outer walkways, the crossing in the middle of the nave, the oval choir for the monks (behind the apses), and Pierre Caqué's façade (1745-50). As late as the reign of Louis XIII, it was used as the court chapel.

34

St-Paul-St-Louis
1627-41
P. Etienne Martellange and P. François Derrand
99, Rue St-Antoine, 4e
Metro: St-Paul

The Jesuits were driven out of Paris from 1595-1603, and did not reestablish themselves fully until 1850. This church, however, became the first modern – that is, inspired by Italian influences – Jesuit church in Paris. Louis XIII himself broke the ground, with Martellange's plans following the model of the Jesuit mother church in Rome. Derrand took over the master architect duties in 1629 and oversaw everything from the laying of the cornerstone for the façade through its eventual completion in 1641. The powerful, festive Baroque façade, adorned with sculptures and double columns, masks the light, blandly colored domed nave with five bays and accompanying domed chapels and galleries between gigantic Corinthian pillars. Above the transept, which itself is not particularly prominent, sits a cupola above an eight-cornered drum room, which is surprisingly unnoticeable on the buildings silhouette. Note the forechoir bay and the semicircular apse, as well as the rich sculpture on the strapwork.

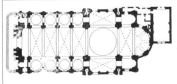

35

Notre-Dame-des-Victoires
1629-1740
Pierre Lemuet and Sylvain Cartault
1, Place des Petits-Pères, 2e
Metro: Bourse

Louis XIII laid the cornerstone for this church –
run by the barefooted Augustinians (called *Augustins
déchaussés* or *Petits Pères*) – in remembrance of the
conquest of La Rochelle (1628). A pillar-covered
gabled façade contrasts the cool, four-bayed,
barrel-vaulted nave, with accompanying chapel,
transept, and deep choir. Although Lemuet drafted the first plans for the building, dire financial
constraints required that Cartault take over the
completion of the project from 1737-40.

36

St-Jacques-du-Haut-Pas
1630 and 1675-83
252, Rue St-Jacques, 5e
Metro: Luxembourg

As early as 1180, there was mention of a hospital with a chapel on this spot, specifically one
run by a Tuscan order from Altopascio on the
pilgrimage path to Santiago de Compostela. A
Benedictine cloister was founded here in 1572,
and the Oratorians moved in 1621. Following
the laying of the cornerstone by Gaston d'Orléans, brother of Louis XIII in 1630, construction began on a polygonal galleried choir to
complement the chapel (built 1584). A transept
and a distinct, soberly lighted nave with half-bar-
rel and cupola vaulting and a noticeable barren
façade were added between 1675 and 1683
(plans by Daniel Gittard, financial help from
Anne G. de Bourbon, Duchess of Longueville, a
known patron of the factor and of the Port-Royal abbey). The asceticism of this church seems
to be a direct retort by the Jansenists to the extravagant tendencies of the aristocratic set.

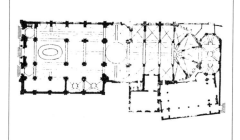

37

Temple Ste-Marie
1632-34
François Mansart
17, Rue St-Antoine, 4e
Metro: Bastille

This church is one of architect François Mansart's early works, built for the "Sisters of the Visitation of Mary" (Visitandines) on their 1619 arrival in Paris, with financial patronage by Jeanne de Chantal. The compact, centralized cupola-crowned structure is a Rome-influenced predecessor to the Val-de-Grâce church, with an arch-framed portal, a square-framed rotunda, (diameter 15 meters, 35 meters high) with a ring of oval chapels and pillars arranged beneath the dome. Typical for Mansart's style are the complex fusion of the spaces and the finely terraced settlement of the planes. The building has served as a Protestant parish church since 1803, with restoration from 1872-74.

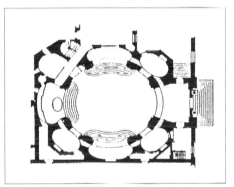

38

Port-Royal Abbey
1625 and 1646-48
Antoine Lepautre
123-125, Boulevard de Port-Royal, 14e
RER: Port Royal

From the Cistercian cloister of Port-Royal-des-Champs from the Chevreuse valley (founded 1204, dissolved ca. 1709-10) came the impetus for the Port-Royal, the highlight of Jansenism. With support from the abbess Angélique Arnauld and help from Jean Duvergier de Hauranne, abbot from St-Cyran, the cloister moved and erected the convent of Port-Royal-de-Paris with Antoine Lepautre's plans. They called for a modest cruciform with shallow arched, pillared arcades.

39

Chapelle Ste-Ursule-de-la-Sorbonne
1627-35
Jacques Lemercier
Place de la Sorbonne, 5e
Metro: Luxembourg

Robert de Sorbon, the court chaplain of Louis IX, built a residence for poor students and professors of theology on this location in 1253. This residence grew quickly and soon engendered an internal system of governance. A chapel was added in 1326 (the spot is marked in the courtyard), and a library followed in 1481. New construction on the ramshackle structure began in 1627 with support from Cardinal Richelieu, who had been the Provisory of the college since 1622. Jacques Lemercier contributed a three-winged structure, which was closed in 1791 and opened again thirty years later as the Humanities center for the university. Between 1885 and 1901, it was replaced by Paul Henri Nénot – chosen by competition – by a much larger scale building (246×83 meters). This new structure featured an eclectic form and a wealth of paintings (including the richly allegorical "Le Bois sacré" by Puvis de Chavannes (1887-89) in the largest of the lecture halls). Lemercier also provided the plans for the chapel, which was to serve as Richelieu's tomb and was built between 1635 and 1648. Lemercier, schooled in Rome, provided a barrel-vaulted Greek cross, with extended eastern and western arms (49 meters each), a high cupola (51 meters), four double-arched, open chapels in the corner of the cross and in the two visible fronts, one on the west and one in the northern transept in the courtyard. Hints of early 17th century Roman design surface in the structure: pure proportions, clear spatial relationships, and restrained decor (cupola artwork by Philippe de Champaigne). Ironically, the tomb of Cardinal Richelieu, who had died in 1642, was only completed in 1694 by François Girardon.

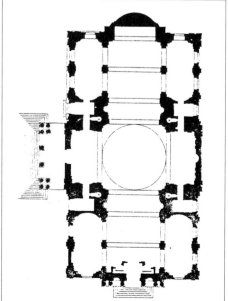

40

Val-de-Grâce
1624-67
François Mansart and Jacques Lemercier
277, Rue St-Jacques, 5e
Metro: Luxembourg

This building, one of the most important Baroque ensembles in the city, originally housed a Benidictine nunnery that was transferred to Paris from Bièvre in 1621, with the first building erected in 1624. Anne d'Autriche had made an oath to God to build a church when a successor to throne was born, and in 1638 Louis le Désiré was born to Louis XIV. Mansart created the first blueprints, overseeing the groundbreaking in 1645, but by 1646 Lemercier had taken over. The construction was halted between 1648 and 1655, but was finally finished in 1667. The consecration did not occur until 1710. The 50 meter long church with a 41 meter high dome actually followed Mansart's original concept closely, with a festive courtyard, flights of steps, a two-story façade with a columned porch, a short nave and three bays with an arrangement of Corinthian pillars, a coffered barrel dome, and domed side chapels. The few changes included the volutes on the upper half of the façade, the rounding off of the domes, and the addition of vaulting without an attica. The choir served as a central structure,

with a three-concha structure in the square accompanied by oval-shaped diagonal chapels, while a richly arranged "Roman" cupola (19 meter diameter) accentuates the altar room. The catacombs held (until the Revolution) the hearts of 47 princes and princesses. Since 1655, all new construction to the cloister has taken place on the southern side – the widow's residence for the queen, planned for the northern side, was never finished. The cloister disbanded in 1790. Restorations took place between 1862 and 1865 and between 1988 and 1990.

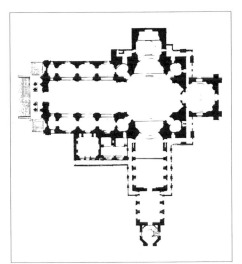

41

St-Sulpice
1634-1736
Christophe Gamard, Louis Le Vau, Daniel Gittard, Gilles-Marie Oppenordt, and Giovanni Niccolò Servandoni (Façade)
Place St-Sulpice, 6e
Metro: St-Sulpice

A parish church named Sulpicius was first built here in 1211, consecrated to the Bishop of Bourges (621-24). Its axis, planned by the master architect Christophe Gamard in 1634, was clearly different from those of the modern church. After the intervention of Curé J.J. Olier, the groundbreaking by Anne d'Autriche was made possible in 1646. Louis Le Vau was commissioned in 1649 to make alterations in the proportions. The construction was taken over in 1670 by Daniel Gittard, whose nave designs would eventually be completed in 1736 by Gilles-Marie Oppenordt. Yet a lack of funds repeatedly halted the construction. A contest was held for façade design, won by the Florentinian theater decorator Giovanni Niccolò Servandoni in 1732, although his plans were not implemented until 1869, and even

then only partially. The church was consecrated in 1745. The church itself is a 120-meter long drummed basilica (30-meter high nave), pleasantly wide with hip-vaulted side aisles, a transept, gallery, and chapel rows. To this light, sober descendant of the Notre-Dame cathedral, Servandoni contributed a powerful façade with a doubled portico ringed with towers (although the gables were never built), an early, austere rebuttal to the Rococo movement. The portico holds allegories of the Virtues and reliefs of the Evangelists, by Michel-Ange Slodtz (1759). There is also a fountain on the broad forecourt by Louis T.J. Visconti (1844).

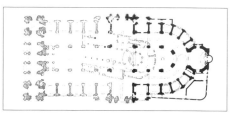

42
St-Roch Parish Church
1653 and 1701-40
Jacques Lemercier, Jules Hardouin-Mansart, Robert de Cotte (Facade), Etienne Maurice Falconet, and Etienne Louis Boullée
298, Rue St-Honoré, 1er
Metro: Palais-Royal

This church represents the sober masterpiece of Baroque church architecture in Paris: it is a light, triple-aisle, barrel-vaulted basilica church of 126 meters in length, with a flat, forward-set transept, a flat cupola, and a choir gallery above a circular chapel based on those at Notre-Dame. Louis XIV broke the ground in 1653, according to plans by Jacques Lemercier. After some delay, construction was resumed in 1701, with a Marian chapel and gallery completed from 1705-10, probably by Jules Hardouin-Mansart. A second eastern chapel was added in 1711, with the addition of the vaulted ceilings in 1723 and the column-studded façade by Robert de Cotte in 1736. Consecration took place in 1740. Builders Etienne Maurice Falconet and Etienne Louis Boullée added a third eastern chapel between 1754 and 1760.

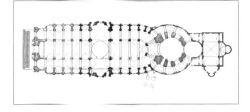

43
St-Nicolas du-Chardonnet
after 1656
François Levé and Michel Noblet
30, Rue St-Victor, 5e
Metro: Maubert-Mutualité

This church, built as a replacement for a chapel of the St-Victor abbey (originally consecrated in 1230), was erected near a post-Gothic tower (1625) after 1656. François Levé and Michel Noblet together designed this modest, triple-aisle, barrel-vaulted parish church, including a transept, choir gallery, and circular chapel (60 meters long). Vaulting was completed in 1763, and the façade dates back only from 1927-37.

44
Hôpital de la Salpêtrière
after 1660
Louis Le Vau
47, Boulevard de l'Hôpital, 13e
Metro: St-Marcel

La Salpêtrière, a powder factory, was built in 1634, just outside of the city. It was transformed in 1656 into a general hospital, later an institution for women and then (beginning in 1684) a prison. A long, sober structure, similar to a cloister, was begun around a courtyard in 1660 by the architect Louis Le Vau. Only the northern side was completed at this time – a southern wing was added in 1765. Noteworthy is the barren chapel by Libéral Bruant (1660-77), an eight-sided altar room with a dome at its center (20 meter diameter). Four halls of approximately 24 meters each occupy the main trunk, with four eight-sided chapels on the diagonals.

45
St-Louis-en-l'Ile
1664-1726
François Le Vau and Gabriel Le Duc
19-end, Rue St-Louis-en-l'Ile, 4e
Metro: Pont Marie

This cruciform church, even with a choir gallery and a chapel subtly inconspicuous from the street, was built as a replacement for a 1622 chapel. Ground was broken in 1664 following plans by Le Vau, although further construction was led by Le Duc. The choir was consecrated in 1679, and the transept and nave followed between 1702 and 1725, with the final consecration in 1726. The church features a harmonic, triple-aisle structure with pillars and a dome.

46

Collège des Quatre-Nations (Institut de France)
1663-91
Louis Le Vau
23, Quai de Conti, 6e
Metro: Pont Neuf

This Baroque ensemble, the most impressive in Paris, was built on a grant from Cardinal Mazarin in 1661 to serve as a college for 60 students from four of France's recently conquered states (Artois from Flanders, Alsace from Germany, Roussillon from Spain, and Piemont from Italy, all in 1648 or 1659).

The designs included a public library and a chapel as grave church. The plans are in the axis of the Cour Carrée of the Louvre, although an originally planned bridge was never completed. François d'Orbay and Pierre Lambert helped with the construction, which engendered the church between 1663 and 1674, the college building in 1688, and the library in 1691. A group of buildings, Roman in inspiration, were erected on the riverside site of the medieval Tour de Nesle, with two-story, pillar-studded wings linking high, rectangular pavilions (one the library, the other the academy) with a cupola church in the center of the semicircular design. Note the gigantic pillars on the portico façade and on the pavilions.

The chapel was a white, festive central building (30×34 meters, in the form of a Greek cross, with an high, oval dome over Corinthian pillars and a rounded choir cupola).

Impassioned monuments to the church's patron, entombed in the chapel in 1684, include a kneeling marble statue, and 3 bronze symbolic figures of Wisdom, Peace, and Faith – all by Antoine Coysevox, with assistance from Jean-Baptiste Tuby, and design by Jules Hardouin-Mansart. The building has been the headquarters of the Institut de France since 1805, which was founded in 1795 as the descendent of the five royal academies. Note the statue of Napoleon, founder of the universities, in an altar niche, sculpted in 1810 by Philippe Roland. Restorations were completed between 1960-62 and in 1974.

47

Hôtel des Invalides / Eglise des Soldats / St-Louis-des-Invalides

1671-74
Libéral Bruant and Jules Hardouin-Mansart
Esplanade des Invalides, 7e

Metro: Varenne

This building, a successor to similar institutions built under Henri IV and Richelieu, was founded by Louis XIV in 1670 as a convalescence facility for 4,000 to 6,000 disabled veterans. After a design contest, this gigantic complex (450×390 meters, with a 196-meter northern façade, 45 axes) was built in 1671-74. It resembles both a castle and a cloister, with 17 courtyards and 17 kilometers of corridors on the level by Grenelle (plans by Libéral Bruant). Similar martial themes recur in the façade of the Cour d'honneur (102×63 meters) and the bright, 70-meter long soldier's church, a drum structure of nine bays with side aisles and galleries. Its plans were probably drafted by Bruant or perhaps even Jules Hardouin-Mansart, who was entrusted in 1676 by Minister of War Louvois to build a choir building for the festival services. The 105-meter high choir (St-Louis-des-Invalides or Eglise Royale, begun in 1679) is a grandiose, domed central building, with its own southern façade, probably intended to be the mausoleum of the Sun King. It is a two-story square (52 meters per side) with an inscribed rotunda at the center of a Greek cross, rounded diagonal chapels, an oval choir, a steep drum base directly on the rotunda walls, and a three-layered cupola.

The cupola was finished in 1690, featuring a fresco of St. Louis created by Charles de la Fosse between 1702-06. The church was consecrated in 1706. Napoleon was interred in 1840 in an open space designed by Louis T.J. Visconti. 1861 saw the erection of a porphyry sarcophagus for the remains of Napoleon. The entire complex has undergone renovations since 1964, with new gilding of the cupola in 1989. The southern side of the complex is noteworthy for its interaction with the city, where it creates a star-formed intersection. The Esplanade (1704-20), by Robert de Cotte, sits on the site of the Pré-aux-Clercs.

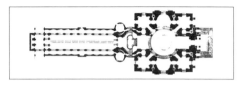

48

Fontaine des Innocents
1547-49
Pierre Lescot
Place Joachim-du-Bellay, 1er
Metro: Les Halles

Architect Pierre Lescot added, at Henri II's request, three viewing balconies onto the face of the ragged Church of the Innocent Children; Jean Goujon later added beautiful reliefs of naiads. Quatremère de Quincy saved this work to complete a fourth arcade and convert it into a free-standing temple. The waterfall steps, the reservoir bowl, and the cupola behind the gables were added in the 19th century.

49

Hôtel Carnavalet (City Museum)
1548-50
Pierre Lescot
23, Rue de Sévigné, 3e
Metro: St-Paul

This first-rate city mansion was built for Jacques des Ligneris, a politician, possibly by Pierre Lescot. The imposing, multi-winged structure encircles a courtyard and features sculptures by Jean Goujon and his workshop, as well as allegorical reliefs of the seasons and the Zodiac on the façades. François Mansart oversaw the respectful expansion which began in 1654, including the addition of more stories to the side wings and the entryway, as well as a new staircase, all commissioned by Claude Boislève. Madame de Sévigné took her residence here from 1677 to 1696, although the building fell into the city's possession in 1866. It has served as the City Museum since 1880, when entire parts of other dilapidated hôtels were transferred to the garden and different room scenes from the 17th and 18th centuries were put on display. The museum now experiences ongoing renovation.

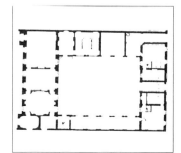

50

Pont Neuf
1578-1607
Jean-Baptiste Androuet Ducerceau and Guillaume Marchant
1er-7e

Metro: Pont Neuf

This is the oldest intact bridge in Paris, made of stone and stretching 233 meters. Henri III broke ground in 1758, although the construction (led by Ducerceau and Marchant) was broken off by the religious wars and was only finished in 1607. The bridge spans the river on two beams, one with 7 arches, the other with 5, and on the point of the Ile de la Cité the bridge widens into an open area for a monument of a mounted Henri IV. Because of the bridge, no one was allowed to build houses on the nearby banks of the Seine, allowing for an undisturbed view of the Louvre. The semicircular bay windows over the pillars initially served as market stands. Also noteworthy is the sidewalk, used here for the first time to allow pedestrians to pass safely and easily over the bridge. The only adornment is a masked frieze down by the waterside. The candelabrum were added in 1854 by Victor Baltard.

51

Hôtel de Lamoignon or d'Angoulême (Historical Library of the City of Paris)
1594-98
Jean-Baptiste Androuet Ducerceau
24, Rue Pavée, 4e

Metro: St-Paul

This Late Renaissance building was designed (perhaps) by Androuet Ducerceau for Diane de France, daughter of Henri II. It features a narrow courtyard, a slender *corps de logis* with exaggerated flanking pavilions, and early examples of gigantic Corinthian pillars supporting an attic, between five-window axes. Two wings were added to the courtyard in 1624, although the southern of the two was removed in 1834.

52
Place des Vosges
1605-12
4e

Metro: Bastille

This plaza, built on the site of Henri IV's Hôtel des Tournelles by designs of either Louis Métezeau or Claude Chastillon, is one of Paris's most important civil achievements. The festive square plan (108 meters per side) leads to 36 individual houses, stretching from the Pavillon de la Reine to the north to the southern Pavillon du Roi, made of bricks and ashlar, each with four arcaded axes, window-doors on the ground floors, and dormers on the hipped roofs. The plaza was renamed Place Royale in 1639 and was adorned with a royal mounted monument (designed for Louis XIII by Richelieu, with a horse from Daniele da Volterra stable and a rider from Pierre Briard, Jr.) After the monument's destruction during the Revolution, a marble statue by J.-P. Cortot and Ch. M. Dupaty was erected as a replacement. The park and fountain date from the 19th century.

53
Place Dauphine
after 1607
1er

Metro: Pont Neuf

This plaza is a paragon of early 19th century civil architecture. Designed as a marketplace, it was named for Louis XIII's heir (b. 1601), although the architect is today unknown. The houses around the plaza are all identical: three stories with two axes, identical façades, and stores on the ground floor below two residence floors. The highly colorful "Brique-et-pierre" construction – brick walls with ashlar frames – was highly typical of that period. The head buildings by the river have been nicely renovated.

54
Hôpital St-Louis
1607-11
Claude Chastillon and Claude Vellefaux
2, Place du Docteur-Alfred-Fournier, 10e
Metro: Colonel Fabien

The medieval Hôtel-Dieu near Notre-Dame was even in Henri IV's time the only large hospital in the city. The Hôpital St-Louis was built by the king between 1607 and 1611, outside the city walls, to handle those stricken with the plague. It features 4 wings with eight pavilions, with a changeover between ashlar and bricks typical for that period, around a square courtyard (120 meters per side). The walled complex, which even includes a vegetable garden, was probably designed by Claude Chastillon, with a vaulted storage room on the ground floor wing and a high sanitarium room above. The chapel, on the western side of the main building, is a barrel vaulted hall with a groin-vaulted transept and semicircular apses. Note Claude Vellefaux's medieval reminiscences (on the pillar struts and on the gable façades). There is a grandstand for the royal couple (embossed with their initials) above the portal. The building, greatly expanded, has been a full-time hospital since 1773.

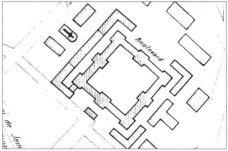

55
Collège de France
after 1611
11, Place Marcelin-Berthelot, 5e
Metro: Maubert-Mutualité

This Humanist research institution was founded by François I in 1530. Guillaume Budé intended the college to counteract the Modernist aesthetic, but also to jar the university, which was locked exclusively into Greek and Hebrew instruction. Louis XIII broke the ground for what is today a four-part complex. The buildings around the festive courtyard were completed between 1774-80 by Jean F. Th. Chalgrin, with expansions by Paul Letarouilly from 1831-42 and by Albert and Jacques Guilbert between 1928-33.

56

Palais du Luxembourg
1615-31 and 19th century
Salomon de Brosse, Jean François Thérèse Chalgrin
15, Rue de Vaugirard, 6e
Metro: Luxembourg

This was the widow's residence of Marie de' Medici, built on land acquired in 1612. Its Early Baroque design is similar in structure to a castle, featuring three wings with pointed pavilions and a terraced gallery with a middle pavilion on the entrance side. Salomon de Brosse was responsible for this part of the construction, with certain Florentinian influences from Palazzo Pitti, such as powerful Mannerist pillars and rustic structures on the outside, with an interior, three-sided arcade court. A cycle of art about the Medicis was originally found in the right wing, painted by Rubens. The gallery for Henri IV in the opposite wing was never finished. The building was used during the Revolution as a weapons plant and a jail. Beginning in 1800, reconstructions were made on behalf of the Senate by Jean François Chalgrin. It has served as the headquarters for the Chambre des Pairs since 1811. The garden side was doubled in size between 1836-41 by Alphonse de Gisors, with the addition of extra space for a throne chamber between 1852-54 in the style of Napoleon's second reign. Note the important paintings by Eugène Delacroix (1845-47) in the reading room of the library.

The building has been the headquarters since 1958 of the "Sénat de la République Française." The president of the senate actually lives in the Petit Luxembourg, which dates back to the original Hôtel of 1546, given over by Marie de' Medici in 1627 to Cardinal Richelieu for serious renovations. Salons were added between 1709 and 1711 by Germain Boffrand. The Jardin de Luxembourg is a park (26 hectometers) with numerous statues and symmetrical French and irregular English pieces. The Fontaine de' Medici, originally a grotto wall from the early 17th century on the example of the Boboli gardens, was converted by Chalgrin into a fountain.

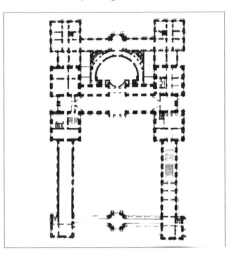

57

Palais-Royal (Conseil d'Etat)
after 1629 and 1752-70
Jacques Lemercier and Pierre Contant d'Ivry
Place du Palais-Royal, 1er
Metro: Palais-Royal

The powerful Palais-Royal, seat of the state council, harkens from the days of Cardinal Richelieu, who, as Prime Minister, commissioned his favorite architect, Jacques Lemercier, to build the royal palace adjacent to the Louvre. From this three-winged complex with an entry court to the south and a forecourt to the north, only the Galerie des Proues remains: a wall with reliefs made of ship's anchors and prows. Richelieu willed his palace to the king, and in 1643 it became the residence of Anne d'Autriche. It was given as a gift in 1692 to the king's brother, the Duke of Orléans. Architect d'Ivry oversaw new construction (still according to Lemercier's plan) from 1752-70, although the sculptural ornamentation on the façade was executed by Augustin Pajou. Philippe-Egalité was responsible for even more expansion, including elegant arcades, stores, and stately manors (sixty 3-axis buildings) by Victor Louis on three sides of the pretty northern garden. The palace was renovated from 1818-30 by Pierre François Léonard Fontaine for Louis Philippe, including the construction of a northern pavilion as well as a connecting gallery, whose glass-covered walkway served as an early shopping arcade. Prosper Chabrol oversaw the removal of damage caused by the Paris Commune from 1872-76. Line artist Daniel Buren's multi-section sculptures have graced the garden since 1985-86, while artist Pol Bury's steel sculptures are found in the fountain. The Théâtre du Palais-Royal (#38 Rue Montpensier) on the northern corner of the long, rectangular garden, damaged by a fire, was restored first in 1830 by Louis Régnier de Guerchy and later in 1887 by Paul Sédille, who added a curious fire escape to the façade.

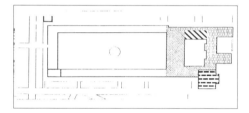

58

Hôtel de Sully
1624-30
Jean-Baptiste Androuet Ducerceau
62, Rue St-Antoine, 4e
Metro: St-Paul

This lavish, Early Baroque palace exemplifies the styles of Louis XIII's reign. Built by Ducerceau, it was later acquired by Maximilian de Béthune, the Duke of Sully. The street façade features powerful pointed pavilions, with a splendid festive courtyard with three opulently decorated wings, as well as a garden with the lowlying palace Petit Sully (both from 1631-41). It is today the headquarters of the Caisse Nationale des Monuments Historiques.

59

Bibliothèque Nationale
17th-19th Century
Jean Thiriot, François Mansart, Armand Claude Mollet, Robert de Cotte, Henri Labrouste, Jean Louis Pascal and Michel Roux-Spitz
58, Rue de Richelieu, 2e
Metro: Palais-Royal

The National Library of France is actually made up of numerous buildings around a collection of courtyards, spread out over 16,500 square meters. The oldest part is the Hôtel Tubeuf, built from brick and ashlar in 1635 by Thiriot for Duret de Chevry and featuring a pretty forecourt. Cardinal Mazarin took residence there in 1641, and the Mazarine Gallery, a two-story gallery wing was added in 1645 by Mansart. The cardinal died in 1661 and the estate was split up. On the northern section, the Scottish banker John Law had a "Galerie Neuve" built, initially by Mollet in 1719 and later (1731) by de Cotte. Particularly noteworthy is the distinctive western façade, today the entry court to the library. Beginning in 1724, the building was extended out to the national library. Labrouste created the rectangular reading room from 1858-68, including exedras, several cupolas on fine cast-iron columns, and a glass partition between the reading room and the stacks. The room is today considered one of the most important early achievements in iron architecture. The extensions were completed around 1875 by Pascal and Roux-Spitz, with a card catalog room added in 1932.

60

Hôtel Lambert
1640-44
Louis Le Vau
2, Rue St-Louis-en-l'Ile, 4e
Metro: Pont Marie

This irregularly shaped hôtel, built on the eastern tip of the St-Louis island for the royal secretary and financier Jean-B. Lambert de Sucy et Thorigny between 1640-44, was considered one of Louis Le Vau's masterpieces. It features a rusticated gatehouse, a three-story wing with half-columns around a rounded-off courtyard, and monumental Ionic pillars on the garden façade. Very little remains of the apartments (Cabinet des Muses, Cabinet de l'Amour) which the architect (d. 1644) built for his brother Nicolas. One exception is the famous "Galerie d'Hercule," a rounded-off hall with 8 windows, gilded wall coverings, twelve bronze reliefs of the "Deeds of Hercules" by Gérard van Obstal, and the Illusionistic painting "Apotheose des Herkules" by Charles Lebrun. The building has been owned by the Rothschild estate since 1976.

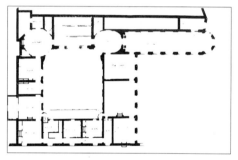

61

Hôtel d'Aumont (Tribunal Administratif)
1645-56
Louis Le Vau, François Mansart
7, Rue de Jouy, 4e
Metro: St-Paul

This important city palace was begun in 1645 by Le Vau. It was actually signed over to the stepson of the architect, Marschall Antoine d'Aumont, in 1656, to be expanded and rebuilt by Mansart. Notable are the gatehouse, ringed by pavilions, the court with three wings of equal height, the changeover from windows to textured fields, and a long (19 axes) façade down to the garden. Some of the ceiling decor has survived.

62

Hôtel de Guénégaud (Musée de la Chasse et de la Nature)
1648-53
François Mansart
60, Rue des Archives, 3e
Metro: Rambuteau

This parcel of land was purchased in 1647 by Jean François de Guénégaud des Brosses, the treasurer of France, and was built by Mansart between 1648 and 1653. It features a gateway with a terrace, side wings, a well-balanced main wing (such proportioning was typical for Mansart), with intricate stonework, especially in the detail work. Because the windows of the house are so large, the house has a see-through effect.

63

Hôtel de Beauvais
1655-60
Antoine Lepautre
68, Rue François-Miron, 4e
Metro: St-Paul

This building was built by Lepautre for Pierre de Beauvais and his wife, one of Anne d'Autriche's ladies-in-waiting. The heavy façade, with seven axes, has lost its original ornamentation, and the main wing now has a store on its ground floor. The curved Baroque court is impressive, with a superposition outlining the different floors, a gallery with terraced gardens over the stables. There is also a rounded vestibule and a staircase with lavish adornment by Martin Desjardins.

64

Hôtel Salé or Aubert de Fontenay
1656-59
Jean Bouiller de Bourges
5, Rue de Thorigny, 3e
Metro: St-Paul

This stately hôtel with a garden and yard was built for Pierre Aubert, Seigneur de Fontenay. Included are a curved gateway, a wide forecourt with a low wing in front of the stall yards, a monumental main façade, a roomy, three-pathed staircase with splendid sculptures. It has been owned by the state since 1962 and was reconfigured in 1981 as a Picasso museum (opened 1985) by Bernard de Vitry.

65

Hôtel Lauzun

1656-57
Louis Le Vau
17, Quai d'Anjou, 4e
Metro: Pont Marie

A paragon of 17th century metropolitan culture, this hôtel presents itself simply on the outside (3 stories, 6 axes, and a balcony), but the inside is much more adorned. Sets of enfilade rooms lay on both floors with wooden paneling, stucco doorways, and artwork based on the function of each room, all of an outstanding quality. It came into the possession of the Count of Lauzan in 1682, but after various ownership, the city acquired the deed in 1928.

66

Hôtel des Ambassadeurs de Hollande or Amelot de Bisseuil

1657-60
Pierre Cottard
47, Rue Vieille-du-Temple, 4e
Metro: St-Paul

This palace was built on the site of the Hôtel des Rieux for J.B. Amelot de Bisseuil. It was planned as an alternative approach to a project begun in 1638. Radical changes were made beginning in 1759 by Louis Le Tellier. Of the extravagant adornment of the 16th century, two survivors are the double-sided tympanum by Perrol and the carved door by Thomas Regnaudin. The hôtel currently houses the Fondation Paul-Louis-Weiller.

67

Hôtel de Tallard or Amelot de Chaillou

1702-04
Pierre Bullet
78, Rue des Archives, 3e
Metro: Hôtel de Ville

Architect Pierre Bullet expanded this house, acquired by Jacques Amelot de Bisseuil in 1658, between 1702-04. It was a corner house with two walls on the corner parcel of land and a staircase porch to the garden, the remains of whose Illusionist wall structure can still be seen. It was sold to the Count of Tallard in 1772 and restored in 1980.

68

Observatory
1667-72
Claude Perrault
61, Avenue de l'Observatoire, 14e
RER: Port-Royal

This observatory, the oldest functional one of its kind, was the first national observatory in France. It was built outside the city limits between 1667 and 1672 by Claude Perrault, a doctor and architect, with the financial support of astronomer A. Auzout and the High Minister of Finances, Jean-Baptiste Colbert. It is a cool, smooth, three-story square block with an angular porch to the north and two octagonal pavilions to the south, a covered terrace, arched windows, and a 28-meter deep, climate controlled cellar for the apertures, as well as prettily vaulted halls and a virtuoso example of a cut-stepped arch. On 21 June, 1667, the building was oriented to the compass points, with the meridian of Paris running through its middle. The observatory is a classic example of the rationalistic drives of the 17th century; in addition to astronomy, it serves as the assembly hall of the Académie des Sciences (founded in 1666) and houses its collections.

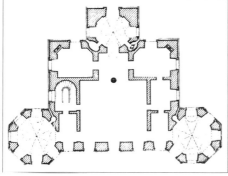

69

Porte St-Denis
1671-73
François Blondel and Michel Anguier
24, Boulevard St-Denis, 2e and 10e
Metro: Strasbourg-St-Denis

This relief-painted triumph arches over one of the main parade routes, on the model of the Titus arch: dedicated by the citizens of the victorious Louis XIV on his return after his maneuvers in Holland (1671-73). Plans for the 23-meter monument, covered with writing on all sides, were completed by Blondel, the founding director of the new Académie de l'Architecture; the sculptor was probably Anguier.

70

Champs-Elysées
after 1667
André Le Nôtre
Metro: Champs-Elysées-Clemenceau

This splendid boulevard dedicated to the Elysian Fields, 3 kilometers long and 71 meters wide, had a predecessor in the Cours-la-Reine, built for Marie de' Medici in 1616. The structure for the grand concourse in the axis of the Tuileries was established in 1667, with the landscaping assignment given to court gardener André Le Nôtre. It has been city-run since 1828, with the last major renovations coming in 1858 by Adolphe Alphand, who surrounded the many alleys with small gardens. Only a few of the many original landmarks along the street remain, including the Restaurant Leydoyen (relocated to its current position in 1848 by Jakob Ignaz Hittorff), the Théâtre Marigny (built by Charles Garnier as a twelve-sided panorama between 1883-84 and changed into a theater in 1893-96), and the Palais des Glaces, built by Gabriel Davioud as the round Théâtre du Rond-Point des Champs-Elysées (40 meter diameter) in 1860.

71

Porte St-Martin
1674
Pierre Bullet
33, Boulevard St-Martin, 3e and 10e
Metro: Strasbourg-St-Denis

Similar to the Porte St-Denis, this smaller (17 meter) and more sober monument to the Sun King was erected on one of the (then) new boulevards. It was dedicated by the lay judges of Paris in 1674 to the conquest of the *Franche-Comté*. Designs came from Pierre Bullet, a student of Blondel's. Louis XIV shines down as Hercules from the spandrel reliefs by Martin Desjardins among others.

72
Hôtel Sagonne-Mansart
1674-85
Jules Hardouin-Mansart
28, Rue des Tournelles, 4e
Metro: Bastille

Hardouin-Mansart, the Count of Sagonne, built this as his own residence from 1674-85. A colonnade was added to the front of the courtyard in 1767. The garden on the Boulevard Beaumarchais (# 21) faces a unique façade, with a continuous balcony whose Ionic double columns run down between the windows of the ground floor. Two gabled balcony foreparts are on the fourth floor. Remains of the original interior decorations can be found inside.

73
Place des Victoires
after 1681-85
Jules Hardouin-Mansart and Martin Desjardins
1er-2e
Metro: Sentier

After the Treaty of Nimwegen in 1679, Louis XIV was at the height of his power, which moved Marschall François d'Aubusson, Duke of La Feuillade, to build him this monument. Martin Desjardins began the 4-meter high bronze statue (with a 7-meter high marble plinth) in 1681, and it was consecrated in 1686 on the horseshoe-shaped plaza (31-meter diameter), which had been planned in 1685 by Jules Hardouin-Mansart on land acquired in

1683 by d'Aubusson. The lavish monument was destroyed in 1792 and later replaced by Napoleon with a naked statue of General L. Desaix. This in turn was replaced by an unexciting mounted figure of Louis XIV by François Joseph Bosio. The bent plaza changeover, with a rusticated ground floor arcade, Ionic monument pillars for 2 living floors, and a mansard roof, has been mostly destroyed by renovations and new streets.

74

Hôtel de Libéral Bruant

1683
Libéral Bruant
1, Rue de la Perle, 3e

Metro: St-Paul

The architect Libéral Bruant acquired this parcel in 1683 and built three adjacent hôtels on
it, the southernmost for himself. It is an ambi-
tious building around a square courtyard, with
a side wing and a curved, two-story *corps de logis* with rounded niches for busts and gables on
top. The city sold it in 1968 to the Société
Bricard, who restored it and installed a "Musée
de la Serrure" in 1976.

75

Place Vendôme

1686-1725
Jules Hardouin-Mansart
1er

Metro: Concorde

This noble plaza, ripe with harmonious and elegant design, was commissioned in 1685 by
Minister Louvois, although a lack of money
delayed its completion until 1725. Its rectangular
design features bevelled corners, a noble façade
with a rusticated ground floor, Corinthian double pillars on both main floors, a mansard
roof, a gabled forepart in the middle of the long
sides and in the corners. A mounted statue of the
king in the vestments of a Roman lord, built in
1699 by François Girardon, was destroyed in
1792. A bronze pillar modeled after Trajan's Column in Rome took its spot, on whose reliefs
Napoleon's exploits in battles of 1805 have
been immortalized. The column, injured during
the Commune Revolt of 1871, was restored two
years later.

76

Amphithéâtre Anatomique
1691-95
Charles and Louis Joubert
5, Rue de l'Ecole-de-Médecine, 6e
Metro: Odéon

Because of their successes, Louis XIV's doctors were granted permission to build an anatomy theater, executed by Charles and Louis Joubert from 1691-95 as a rectangle with an octagonal tambour and dome, with a lavish portal to the street covered by masterful decoration. Before an art school was installed in 1977, the theater served (beginning in 1933) as a lecture room for the Institute of Modern Languages.

77

"Oldest" House in Paris
17th century
3, Rue Volta, 3e
Metro: Arts et Métiers

This house, long believed to date back to 1300 and hence be the oldest in Paris, was in 1979 through newly-discovered documents actually proven to have been built only in the 17th century. It retains many interesting aspects nevertheless, since its construction plan draws overtly from medieval models. a massive ashlar ground floor with 2 shops; a central entrance to steep staircase; a 4-story, smooth buttressed top with perpendicular balconies; and 4 rooms per floor.

78

Hôtel de Brancas
ca. 1700
Pierre Bullet
6, Rue de Tournon, 6e
Metro: Odéon

This noble hôtel with three wings around a courtyard was built around 1700 by Pierre Bullet for Jean Gaston Baptiste Terrat, the Marquis de Chantosme. Especially noteworthy is the pretty marble staircase. The hôtel has held some of the offices of the French Institute of Architecture since 1979.

79

Hôtel de Soubise (National Archives)
1704-09
Pierre Alexis Delamair
60, Rue des Francs-Bourgeois, 3e
Metro: Rambuteau

François de Rohan, prince of Soubise, bought the land for this stately building in 1700, although Delamair did not begin construction until 1704. Note the gigantic forecourt with a double-pillared colonnade and the two-story *corps de logis* with a gabled forepart and sculptural adornment by Robert Le Lorrain. Germain Boffrand expanded and redecorated the building between 1732-39, including the rococo decorations in the princess's bedroom and in the glazed "oval salon."

80

Hôtel de Rohan-Strasbourg / Minutier Central
1705-08
Pierre Alexis Delamair
87, Rue Vieille-du-Temple, 3e
Metro: St-Paul

This city mansion was built by Delamair for the Strasbourg prince's bishop, Armand G. Max de Rohan. Its design includes three wings with a forecourt, a *corps de logis*, and a garden. The interior, which is now a section of the National Archives, has been changed, including restorations from 1928-38. Note the masterpiece of French rococo sculpture above the stable entrance: *Trough of Apollo's Horses*, by Robert Le Lorrain (1731-38).

81

Hôtel Amelot de Gournay
1712
Germain Boffrand
1, Rue St-Dominique, 7e
Metro: Solférino

Architect Germain Boffrand acquired this land in 1712 to begin the construction of a hôtel which he sold in 1713 to the Michel Amelot de Gournay, a diplomat. Its design features a circular courtyard, a *corps de logis* of only five axes, with oversized pilasters, low wings, and a puffed-out middle salon near the garden.

82

Palais d'Elysée
1718-22
Armand Claude Mollet
55-57, Rue du Faubourg-St-Honoré, 8e
Metro: Champs-Elysées-Clemenceau

This residence, highly reminiscent of a castle with its courtyard and garden, was built by Mollet for Henri Louis de la Tour d'Auvergne. It is rectangular (11 axes and two stories) with a central niche, corner pavilions, long, low side wings and a portal to the street framed by double columns. In addition to the many 18th and 19th century rooms, the Op-Art dining rooms, built in 1972 by Pierre Paulin, are well worth seeing. It has been the President headquarters since 1874.

83

Arsenal
1718-45
Germain Boffrand
1-3, Rue de Sully, 4e
Metro: Sully-Morland

Little remains of this site's original occupant, a gunpowder and weapons factory built ca. 1594 by the Duke of Sully for Henry IV. The exterior of this long, three-story barracks was altered in both the 18th century and in the 19th century. Inside, two richly decorated rooms remain near the stairs, a bedroom and workroom/oratorium, completed between 1637 and 1640 by the workshop of Simon Vouet.

84

Hôtel Delisle-Mansart
beginning of 18th century
Pierre Delisle-Mansart
22, Rue St-Gilles, 3e
Metro: Chemin Vert

This small hôtel, with a courtyard, a five-axis main building, a garden, and a pretty portal between its two pavilions, was created by Pierre Delisle-Mansart (d. 1720) at the beginning of the 18th century using pieces of the existing building.

85
Hôtel de Gouffier de Thoix
1719-27
56, Rue de Varenne, 7e
Metro: Varenne

The industrialist Baudouin built this hôtel with its magnificent portal, courtyard, and *corps de logis* for the Marquise de Thoix. The 18th century salon and dining room are particularly noteworthy.

86
Hôtel de Charost
1722-25
Antoine Mazin
39, Rue du Faubourg-St-Honoré, 8e
Metro: Champs-Elysées-Clemenceau

This dignified palace was built by Antoine Mazin of Marseille, a military engineer, for Duke Paul-François de Charost-Béthune, and includes a portal wall, a forecourt, and a two-story *corps de logis*. The interior features numerous elegant, colorfully decorated rooms from the era of Paolina Borghese (1803-14). The British Embassy has been centered here since 1825.

87
Hôtel de Noirmoutiers
1722-23
Jean Courtonne
136, Rue de Grenelle, 7e
Metro: Varenne

This hôtel by Jean Courtonne replaced an earlier house from the late 17th century. Built for Antoine-François de la Trémoille, Duke of Noirmoutiers, it features a *corps de logis* with seven axes, a balcony, and especially fine sculpturing. The interior was modernized and a wing was added in the beginning of 1734. Since 1970, it has served as the headquarters for the prefect of the Ile-de-France region.

88

Palais Bourbon (Assemblée Nationale)
1722-28
Lorenzo Giardini, Pierre Lassurance, Jacques V.
Gabriel and Jean Aubert
128, Rue de l'Université, 7e
Metro: Solférino

With its richly characteristic pillared front towards the river and the Quai d'Orsay, the headquarters of the French National Assembly dates back to a palace commissioned by Louise Françoise de Bourbon, a daughter of Louis XIV and Mme de Montespan. Planned by Lorenzo Giardini (d. 1722), it was actually built between the years of 1722-28 by Pierre Lassurance (d. 1724), Jacques V. Gabriel, and Jean Aubert, with an entrance to the Rue de l'Université and a garden to the Seine. It was acquired in 1756 by Louis XV, sold off in 1764, and then vastly reconstructed by Louis Joseph de Bourbon, Prince of Condé, who (beginning in 1765) added on more stories and additional wings, and united it with its neighboring building, the Hôtel de Lassay (which itself had been built from 1722-28 according to plans by Giardini). It was confiscated in 1792 and rebuilt by Guy de Gisors and Etienne Charles Lesconte into a Parliament. A porch with a twelve-column peristyle was added for Napoleon from 1803-07 to serve as

a counterpiece to Bernard Poyet's Madeleine church. The gabled relief, entitled "France Collecting the Genius of Human Deeds between Order and Strength" was created by Jean-Pierre Cortot from 1839-41, and the four sculptured figures of Sully, L'Hospital, d'Aguesseau, Colbert were done in 1838. The many magnificent, lavishly decorated chambers include: the "Salon de la Paix" with its Illusionist ceiling paintings from 1838 by Horace Vernet; the "Salon Delacroix" with wall and ceiling work, begun in 1838 by Eugène Delacroix; the Assembly Hall, with Jules de Joly's sculptural additions (1829-32), including the statues "Freedom" and "Public Order"; the library with romantic ceiling paintings such as the "History of Ancient Civilization," executed from 1838-47 by Eugène Delacroix and his students.

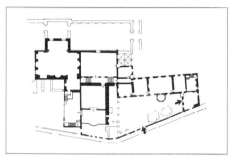

89

Hôtel de Roquelaure
1695-1724
Jean Lassurance
246, Boulevard St-Germain, 7e
Metro: Rue du Bac

This hôtel, begun in 1695 for Duke Antoine Gaston de Roquelaure, was raised in height and incorporated into a powerful new building in 1724 by architect Jean Lassurance. It features a large courtyard with a nine-axis *corps de logis* and pavilion-style wings, as well as numerous rooms with gilded rococo paneling. It is today the seat of the Secretary of State.

90

Hôtel de Loménie de Brienne
1724
François Debias-Aubry
14, Rue St-Dominique, 7e
Metro: Solférino

This charming house was commissioned to architect François Debias-Aubry by the versatile Président Duret for the Marquise de Prie. Completed in 1724 and already sold off by 1725, it features *corps de logis* only two rooms deep, 7 axes, two floors, a gabled center forepart, and a prettily sculptured keystone. It was bought in 1776 by Count Brienne, and was acquired by the government in 1817. Today it is a part of the Ministry of Defense.

91

Hôtel Chenizot
1620-30 and 1719-32
51, Rue St-Louis-en-l'Ile, 4e
Metro: Pont Marie

This house was built for Pierre de Verton, the Secretary of State, between 1620 and 1630. It has one wing facing the street and another between the courtyard and the garden. Its façade was redecorated between 1719 and 1732 for the tax collector François Guyot de Chenizot. The balcony with the dragon-motif console was built in 1727 from designs by Pierre de Vigny.

92

Hôtel Biron (Musée Rodin)
1728-31
Jacques V. Gabriel and Jean Aubert
77, Rue de Varenne, 7e
Metro: Varenne

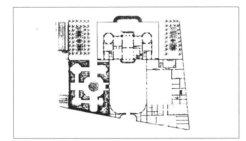

This distinguished, freestanding house, resembles a castle as it sits in a park. It was built as a project of Jacques V. Gabriel (with help from Jean Aubert) for financier and social climber Abrahem Peyrenc of Moras. Its rectangular, two-story design holds double apartments, with 11 axes to the yard and 9 to the garden, as well as corner pavilions and a central forepart, and delicate rococo decor. The stairwell is original, but the room was first outfitted in 1736 in the style of Nicolas Pineau. It is named for the Duke of Biron, the owner from 1753-88. It was used as an artistic workshop beginning in 1905, and Auguste Rodin moved in around 1908; a museum dedicated to his works was erected here in 1919.

93

Hôtel de Braque
after 1673
4-6, Rue de Braque, 3e
Metro: Rambuteau

This double palace was built in the beginning of 1673 for Thomas Lelièvre, Marquis de la Grange, to meet specific measurements. Expensive rococo decor on the façade and in the vestibule, with a balcony atop statuesque consoles and trellises and mascarons in the yard.

94

Hôtel du Grand Veneur
after 1733
Jean-Baptiste Beausire
60, Rue de Turenne, 3e
Metro: Chemin Vert

This house, originally built in 1636, was heavily expanded and redone in the 16th century. It was acquired in 1733 by Augustin Vincent Hennequin, Marquis d'Ecquevilly, who employed Jean-Baptiste Beausire to beautify it. His efforts produced the hunt-related reliefs on the façades and at the foot of the elegant staircase at the rear right of the courtyard, drawing from the owner's position as a General-Captain of the Royal *Vénerie*. It was restored in 1994.

95

Fontaine des Quatre-Saisons
1739-47
Edme Bouchardon
57-59, Rue de Grenelle, 7e
Metro: Rue du Bac

This monument, a bending wall with side passages, sits in a very narrow street. It is two stories high, with a rusticated plinth, pilaster walls, and niches with weapons and figures of the four seasons. A goddess of the city sits enthroned between two river goddesses (for the Seine and Marne) on a central forepart before an aedicula. This decorative masterpiece was created by Edme Bouchardon between 1739-47; its consecration came in 1749. The powerful framework, a product of the "return to antiquity" movement, contrasts strikingly with the rococo figures.

96

Private Residence
1740-50
4, Rue Monsieur-le-Prince, 6e
Metro: Odéon

This simple plaster building (2 axes, 4 floors) features a delightful rococo portal from around 1740-50; its stone frame is capped with a Minerva bust, with masks for volutes on the windows above, and a finely cut double door.

97

Hôtel Clermont-Tonnerre
1714-15
Claude-Nicolas Le Pas-Dubuisson
118-120, Rue du Bac, 7e
Metro: Rue du Bac

In order to take financial advantage, the Congrégation des Missions Etrangères gave permission in 1713 for a parcel of its land to be developed. Builder Le Pas-Dubuisson created a double-house between a court and a garden, intended to be rented out. Both houses had 3 axes around a narrow yard and 7 axes to the garden. Note the rococo casement and the frame on the portals, including four partial images of the world, probably from Jean-Bernard Tureau dit Toro.

98

Hôtel d'Albret
1740-44
Jean-Baptiste Vautrain
31, Rue des Francs-Bourgeois, 4e
Metro: St-Paul

The oldest part of this house (encircling a yard from 1640) contains a distinctive two-story, 7-axis façade with a central entrance, built from 1740-44 according to plans by Jean-Baptiste Vautrain for the President of Parliament, Charles du Tillet, Marquis de La Bussière. It has been city-owned since 1975 and was restored in 1983.

99

Private House
18th century
57, Rue du Seine, 6e
Metro: Mabillon

This pretty house with three axes and 4 stories (Melki Gallery) provides a fine example of the Louis Quinze style of adornment with masks and bars.

100

Ecole Militaire
1751-67
Jacques-Ange Gabriel
1, Place Joffre, 7e
Metro: Ecole Militaire

This monument to the exploits of Louis XV was intended by its sponsors–Joseph Pâris-Duverney, a military supplier, and the Marquise de Pompadur–as a military academy for 500 disadvantaged cadets. The building commenced in 1751 according to plans by Jacques-Ange Gabriel, although it was halted due to the Seven Year War and was also sharply curtailed between 1768-82. The façade side was initially oriented towards the Champs de Mars, but in 1767 it was instead turned to the south. The attractive latticework was created by Fayet. The complex resembles a castle, with pavilions and wings that draw on the Cour Carrée of the Louvre. It also sports a majestic stairwell and chapel to St. Louis (1769-73) with reliefs and paintings. Alexandre Théodore Brongniart added a low wing on the northern side around 1872, although the school and the guard barracks disbanded in 1787. Since 1878 it has housed the Ecole Supérieure de Guerre.

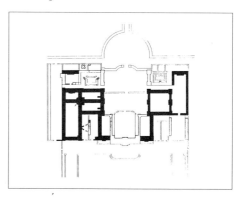

101

Hôtel de Montmor
1751
79, Rue du Temple, 3e

Metro: Rambuteau

This lavish house surrounds two courtyards and was built by the financier Jean Habert de Montmor in 1623 on the site of four existing houses. It was sold in 1751 to tax collector Laurent Charron, whose son oversaw renovations, including three simple, elegant, high, and richly glazed stories. A passageway (1840) ruins the second courtyard, although the main staircase merits note.

102

Place de la Concorde
after 1755
Jacques Ange Gabriel
8e

Metro: Concorde

This grandiose royal 18th century plaza was the last to be built in the city, planned to the west of the Tuileries gardens in 1748 (on land granted by the king) as a mounted monument to Louis XV after his peace accord in Aachen. Gabriel won the commission in 1755 after two contests; his design promised a bridge, an eight-sided plaza open on three sides, and two head buildings to the north (right side: Garde-Meuble, today the Marine Ministry; left: columned façade identical to the colonnade of the Louvre, fronting four houses) and a grand street, the Rue Royale. The statue was erected in 1763 by Edme Bouchardon (later destroyed in 1792), and the bridge was built by J. Rodolphe Perronet from 1788-91. The Rue Royale was not finished until after 1800. In 1836, a 13th century B.C. obelisk captured in Luxor was erected on the spot as a gift to Louis Philippe from Jean-Baptiste Lebas. A fountain with figurines was added between 1836 and 1846 by Jakob Ignaz Hittorff, and in 1838, a sculpture of the goddess of the city was placed atop the watchhouse, fulfilling plans of 1795. The various dangerous dry ditches around the plaza were filled in around 1854. Notice the "Horse Tamer" at the entrance to the Champs-Elysées, by Guillaume Coustou (1745) from Marly castle's park.

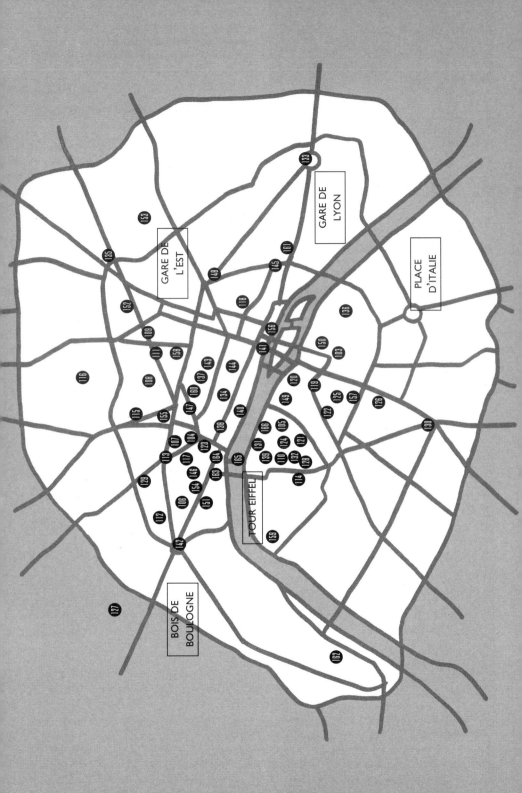

GARE DE LYON

GARE DE L'EST

PLACE D'ITALIE

TOUR EIFFEL

BOIS DE BOULOGNE

Religious and Secular Buildings from Classicism through Art Nouveau

Louis XV (1715-74), the successor to the Sun King, oversaw the expansion of the city. The Place de la Concorde was built in 1755, the Pantheon in 1764, and the Ecole Militaire in 1765. The French capital became the hub of European intellectualism, including the center of criticism against the "ancien Régime." Literature and scientists began to speak out against the arbitrary power of the King, instead promoting a rationalistic ordering of the world. The seminal Encyclopédie des sciences et des arts was compiled by Diderot and D'Alembert from 1751-80.

Shortly after the middle of the century, stark, simple forms were integrated into interior decoration. They also emerged on mansion façades, such as the Hôtel du Châtelet, Hôtel de Cassini, and Hôtel de Massa. The paragons of this new Classical style were the Hôtel d'Alexandre, the Hôtel d'Hallwyl, and the buildings of Alexandre Théodore Brongniart and Pierre Rousseau, which faced the form-overload of rococo with the subtle elegance and strong symmetry of ancient models.

The buildings of the Revolution-era were largely ephemeral, although they drew upon the stability of the Napoleonic style. One ratified urban design, for example, could not be implemented without first completing an earlier Napoleonic city plan.

Louis Philippe (1830-48), as the last king of France, refocused the power to the nobility of France, but the Second Empire, led by the government of Prefect Georges Eugène Haussmann, brought yet another new vision for the city. The Opera (begun in 1860 by Charles Garnier) became synonymous with the Belle Epoque. Its "Style Napoleon III" can be seen today as screaming proof of the pompous tastes of that era's bourgeois.

103

Pantheon

1757-64
Jacques Germain Soufflot
Place du Panthéon, 5e
Metro: Luxembourg

Highly visible atop the Mons Luticius, this domed church boasts of a long history: the site first held a Roman shrine, followed by a church to St. Peter and St. Paul (financed by Clovis in 510). St. Genovefa (d. 512) was also entombed in that structure. She had been a savior of the city against the Huns and the Franks and was made the patron saint of the city and the country in the 9th century, the first female to receive such honors. The Early Classical building owes its existence to an oath by Louis XV. Plans were drawn in 1757 and ground was broken in 1764. Construction was forced to halt when Maximilian Brébion and Jean-Baptiste Rondelet replaced the individual piers on the transept crossing with wall pillars, which made the cupola supports unstable, but the enormous building (100×84 meters) managed to open in 1800. A powerful Greek cross before the cupola (supported by a colonnade) stands out in front of the bare, multi-chamber crypt. This design draws from St. Peter's church in Rome, St. Paul's in London, as well as the Invalid Cathedral, with high plinths, a 22-column portico (modeled on the Roman Pantheon), gabled reliefs, a smoothly sectioned exterior with a festooned frieze and circular cornice, towers flanking the choirs, and a three-layered cupola (83 meters high). The inner space holds 52 elegant, freestanding fluted Corinthian pillars and 72 engaged pillars which frame a peristyl atop the pedestal, all beneath a decorated architrave which bears diversely-styled vaulting in the arms of the cross. The shrine for the church's patrons was intended to stand beneath the cupola. Instead, the church was converted into a "Pantheon," that is, a grave church for the "great men of this era of liberty." Antoine Chrysostome Quatremère de Quincy executed many of these changes, which sharply altered the effect of many of the rooms, including the closure of 42 of the massive windows, the sealing of the entrances in the transepts, and the demolition of the upper story of the choir tower. A bright, Antique-style hall of columns was converted into a cool, enclosed grave building, a church changed into a monumental mausoleum of "Revolutionary architecture." After several attempts to convert the building back to a church, it was firmly established in 1885 as "Pantheon." Soufflot oversaw the conversion of the plaza and the rerouting of the streets from the Garden of Luxembourg.

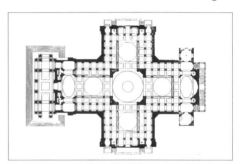

104

Ste-Madeleine

after 1763

Pierre Contant d'Ivry, Guillaume M. Couture and Pierre A. Vignon

Place de la Madeleine, 8e

Metro: Madeleine

The construction of this freestanding, temple-style church suffered many complications. Intended as a replacement for a 13th century Magdalene chapel, ground was broken at the end of the Rue Royale by Louis XV in 1763.

The initial plans by Pierre Contant d'Ivry (d. 1777) called for a Latin cross design with a dome, but after his death, new designs by Guillaume M. Couture called for a Greek cross. In 1791, construction was halted, and plans were made to convert the building into a stock exchange or a similar institute of the Empire. The idea was raised in 1806 of finishing the building as a temple in honor of the Napoleonic army, with Pierre A. Vignon winning the design contest.

Nevertheless, in 1813 the focus shifted back to a church, with Vignon (d. 1828) restarting construction in 1816 on an expiatory church for Louis XVIII.

Accordingly, figure niches were added to the outer wall of the cella by Jean-J.M. Huvé, and it was completed as a parish church in 1842. At 108×43×30 meters with 4 meter plinths and a peripteros of 52 Corinthian columns (each 15 meters high), the temple was both impressive and imposing.

The gable included the work "Le Pardon accordé à la Madeleine" from 1833 by Philippe H. Lemaire, and Henri de Triqueti's bronze door from 1837 displayed reliefs of the ten commandments.

The niches contained 32 patron saints by various leading sculptors.

The interior encompassed a vestibule and three cupola bays with stand-alone columns in front of engaged columns, similar to a marbled Roman caldarium. The choir holds a mosaic from 1893 with a history and glorification of Christianity by Jules Ziegler; it was originally the apse artwork. A masterful tribute to the ascension of Magdalene graces the altar, by Carlo Marochetti (1837).

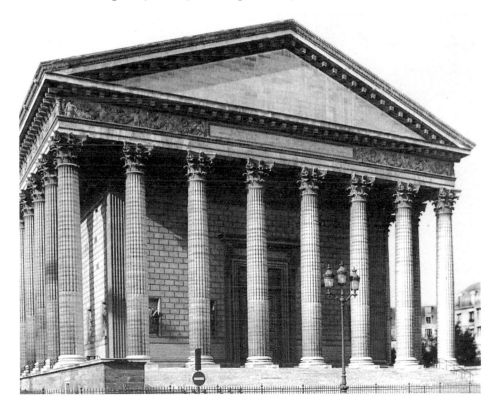

105

St-Thomas-d'Aquin
1683
Pierre Bullet
Place St-Thomas d'Aquin, 7e
Metro: Rue du Bac

Of three Dominican establishments in Paris, only this one, the last built, has preserved. The church, a substitute for the planned chapel, was erected in a mere nine months (plans by Bullet), although two of the western bays and the façade were not finished at the time of consecration. The façade was actually finished between 1765 and 1770 by the monk Claude. The gabled front is in the style of the Counter-reformation, with a two-story column structure. The main church has three aisles and four bays, capped by a bare barrel vault over Corinthian pillars, with flat cupolas over the side bays; a short transept; and a semi-circular apse with a view of the monk's choir from 1722. The cloister was dissolved in 1793 and the building has been used as a parish church since 1803. The cloister from 1735-40 is now an Army administration building.

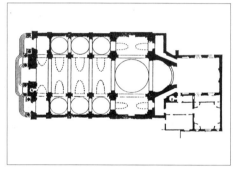

106

St-Philippe-du-Roule
1774-84
Jean François Thérèse Chalgrin
154, Rue du Faubourg-St-Honoré, 8e
Metro: St-Philippe-du-Roule

This parish church from Chalgrin (built according to plans from 1768) is the first example of the incorporation of early Christian architectural motifs into an 18th century French church. The gable of the Doric portico features a "Religio" by Francisque Joseph Duret, while the main building is a dim, three-aisle basilica with 7 bays, with an Ionic colonnade and wood vaulting over the nave and side aisles.

107

Chapelle Expiatoire
1816-26
Hippolyte Lebas and Pierre François Léonard Fontaine
Square Louis-XVI-29, Rue Pasquier, 8e
Metro: St-Augustin

This Late Classical expiatory church was built on an existing Magdalenian graveyard, where the victims of the guillotine on the Place de la Concorde had been interred and whose graves the royalist Descloseaux had previously spared from exhumation. It is a standard Restorationist work, built for Louis XVIII, with a rectangular arcade court before the squared, bare cupola church, three apsis, and a Doric portico above a freestanding staircase.

108

Notre-Dame-de-Lorette
1823-26
Hippolyte Lebas
18bis, Rue de Châteaudun, 9e
Metro: Notre-Dame-de-Lorette

Modeled on designs from the Cesarean era, this church was built by Hippolyte Lebas from 1823-36 on the site of a 17th century chapel in the new Nouvelle Athens district. It is a five-aisle, Ionic column architrave basilica (80×37×27 meters) with a flat room and domed chapels at the head and foot of the side aisles, accompanied by a square choir with a semicircular apse. The Corinthian columns of the portico form a tympanum with an allegory "Mary with Angels", by Charles-Fr. Lebœuf-Nanteuil), as well as three statues (Faith, Love, and Hope). The church is unusually well furnished, including allegorical paintings (such as "The Life of Mary," modeled on the Italian Early Renaissance), pulpits, baptismal fonts, and to trellises.

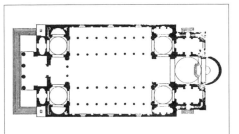

109

St-Vincent-de-Paul
1831-44
Jakob Ignaz Hittorff
Place Franz-Liszt, 10e
Metro: Poissonnière

This church, the most important from the era
of the bourgeois kings, was built as a parish
church for the Poissonnière quarter on the site
of a 12th century leper hospital which had
been taken over in 1620 by St. Vincent of Paul
as a seminary. The initial commission went to
Jean-Baptiste Lepère in 1823, but was taken over
by Ignaz Hittorff, who oversaw the construction
(using different plans) which combined an
early Christian nave with a Greek temple façade.
Highlights include an exposed positioning, iron
stairs, and an Ionic portico in front of a double-
towered façade; plans for polychromatic painting on the exterior were never fulfilled. The layout is a five-aisle, Ionic columned architrave
basilica with 12 bays, each with an elevation and
an exposed roof truss, with coffered ceilings
above the aisles. Behind the triumph arch, the
exterior rows of columns resume in the choir
room. The lavish decoration follows Hittorff's
vision of polychromaticism and the unity of art.

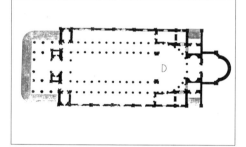

110

Basilica Ste-Clothilde-Ste-Valère
1846-57
Franz Christian Gau
23bis, Rue Las-Cases, 7e
Metro: Solférino

This first neo-Gothic church in Paris – built by the
German architect Gau (d. 1853) – took the form
of a 13th century Gothic church. It is named for
St. Clothilde, the wife of Clovis I, as well as the
martyr Valerie. Features include a twin-towered
façade, which was altered at its completion by
Théodore Ballu, a portico, a nave with six bays
(dry, three part design, with an arcade, a flat triforium, and a loft), a transept, and a choir with
five circular choirs in the style of a cathedral choir.

111

St-Eugène-Ste-Cécile
1854-55
Louis Auguste Boileau and Louis Adrien Lusson
4, Rue du Conservatoire, 9e
Metro: Bonne-Nouvelle

This revolutionary metal structure with a traditional shell was built as a parish church for the Poissonnière quarter on the site of the Hôtel des Menus-Plaisirs by architect Louis Auguste Boileau and engineer Louis Adrien Lusson. However ordinary the rectangular (50×20 meters) neo-Gothic exterior might seem, that more striking is the interior of this three-aisle basilica, with four 23-meter high double bays (rounded windows and 6 ribbed vaults), 4-part vaulting in the side aisles, continuous chapels with low roofs beneath elevations with pointed barrel vaulting, and three polygonal apses. The materials for this inexpensive, screened building – cast and wrought iron – allow for a continuous dematerialization of the walls. The delicate sculptures draw from 13th and 14th century Gothic design. The color period decoration is crucial for the overall effect, including stained glass windows of the life of Christ, ornamental paintings, altars, communion benches, pulpits, and chandeliers.

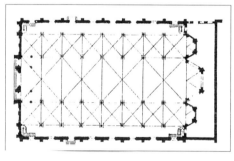

112

St-Alexandre-Nevsky
1859-61
Roman I. Kusjmin and J.B. Strom
12, Rue Daru, 8e
Metro: Ternes

This Russian Orthodox cathedral, consecrated to the national Saints of Russia who died in 1263, replaced an existing chapel and was initiated by embassy priest Joseph Wassiliew. The design stems from the czarist-Russian architects Roman I. Kusjmin and J.B. Strom: a Greek cross with apses, pyramidal groups of towers with small, gilded cupolas. The wall painting program is very rich with Greek Orthodox iconography, iconostasis, a bishop's stool, and numerous icons.

113

St-Augustin
1860-71
Victor Baltard
Place St-Augustin, 8e
Metro: St-Augustin

This freestanding church with an acutely tapered design holds a wealth of architectural history in its momentous exterior and its metallic interior. It was built by Baltard to fit into its "new, gentile quarter," with a gabled façade (including a portico, "King's Gallery" of Christ and the 12 apostles, arched windows in the slender niches on the outside, and arcades, elevations, a loft, and flat cross-vaulting serving the delicate cast and wrought iron decorations on the interior). Note the powerful choir (50 meters high, 25 meters in circumfer-

ence), and the main hall with a cupola and 4 corner towers. The decorative motifs derive strongly from the Italian Renaissance.

114

St-François-Xavier
1861-74
Louis Adrien Lusson and Joseph Uchard
12, Place Président-Mithouard, 7e
Metro: St-François-Xavier

The imposing church of the Historicism movement was begun by Adrien Lusson, who died in 1864, and finished after a design change by Joseph Uchard (consecration in 1874). The twin-towered façade still shows an axis which could not be built out, a façade, a five-aisle main church, a transept, and a triple-aisle choir with elevations, chapel rows, and apses.

115
Trinity Church
1861-67
Théodore Ballu
Place d'Estienne-d'Orves, 9e
Metro: Trinité

Based on a decision by Prefect Haussmann, this parish church was built by Ballu in the style of the French Renaissance (St-Eustache): oval atrium, carriage path with three fountains, façade with a portico, groups of allegorical sculptures, a 65-meter high central tower, a 90-meter long, 30-meter high room with 4 double-bays, flanked by narrow side rows and chapels beneath elevations, barrel vaulting, and a raised choir above the crypt with a colonnade and polygonal apses.

116
Basilique du Sacré-Cœur
1875-1919
Paul Abadie Jr.
Place de Parvis-du-Sacré-Cœur, 18e
Metro: Abbesses

This domed church dates back to the decision by patriotic Catholics Alexandre Félix Legentil and Hubert Rohault de Fleury in December of 1870 to build a monument to the holy heart of Christ and to the "Glory of France and the Rescue of Pope Pious X, who has been taken prisoner in Rome." On the urging of the Jesuits and bishops, the French National Assembly approved this *Vœu national* in 1873, which allowed the forty million Francs cost to be defrayed by the carving of sponsor's initials into the very stones of the church. After an intense competition involving 78 architects, ground was broken in 1875, and the first part was consecrated in 1886 (final consecration in 1919). The church was a substantial (85×35 meters, with an 84-meter cupola) Roman Byzantinian pilgrim's church in the midst of a medieval quarter. Its freestanding stairs acted as a plinth before its crypt, and its foyer was flanked by two mounted statues, one of Joan of Arc and the other of St. Louis (both from 1927 by Hippolyte Lefebvre). The cruciform central hall supported a high central dome and 4 lower sub-cupolas, a choir gallery with a circular choir and a bell tower (1905-10 by Lucien Magne).

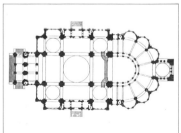

117

Hôtel Alexandre
1763-66
Etienne Louis Boullée
16, Rue de la Ville-l'Evêque, 8e
Metro: Madeleine

Revolutionary architect Boullée built but one house in Paris, this hôtel in the courtyard of the Bank La Hénin, built for André Alexandre, a banker. Note the unusual ashlar façade, with Corinthian pilasters on plinth bases facing the garden, freestanding steps toward the yard, and an open vestibule with 4 columns and 4 side doors beneath oval windows, with a attica floor slightly recessed.

118

Hôtel d'Hallwyl
after 1766
Claude Nicolas Ledoux
28, Rue Michel-le-Comte, 3e
Metro: Rambuteau

The design of this early project by the revolutionary architect includes a stark, two-story street front with banded rustication, a Doric portal with figuring in the tympanum, a courtyard, a blockish main building (3 axes, 3 floors) with corner pavilions, rusticated walls, windows without frames, and low-set side wings. The decor of the second courtyard has disappeared, leaving only the Doric column chains and the nymphaeum. Restorations were completed in 1989 and 1990.

119

Faculté de Médecine
1769-86
Jacques Gondouin
12, Rue de l'Ecole-de-Médecine, 6e
Metro: Odéon

The Surgical Academy was built on the site of the Collège de Bourgogne, founded 1331, and of a Premonstratensian chapel. Gondouin was commissioned by Louis XV to fulfill this project as part of a larger endeavor, the "return to classic antiquity." The results are an Ionic colonnade topped with a half-story on the street side and a courtyard with three wings, the middle of which is a six-columned portico. Additional construction was carried out by Paul Ginain between 1878 and 1900.

120

La Monnaie
1771-77
Jacques Denis Antoine
11, Quai de Conti, 6e
Metro: Cité

This former Royal mint, built on the site of the Hôtel de Conti, provides an excellent example of early Classicism. Louis XV made the decision to build a fresh structure, and Antoine was chosen through contest. His building was a 117-meter long rectangle with 3 floors, 27 subtly harmonious axes, a center forepart emphasized by 6 gigantic Ionic columns, a semicircular, closed-off main courtyard (35×30 meters), and allegorical sculptures. The vestibule is a three-aisled Doric peristyle, while the elegant main stairwell features coffering on pillars. The functional parts of the mint were moved to Pessac in 1973, although a Museum of Money is run in the salons, with various changing exhibitions in the main halls.

121

Hôtel de Cassini
1771-73
Claude B. Bélisard and Pierre Lemonnier
32, Rue de Babylone, 7e
Metro: Sèvres-Babylone

This noble house between a courtyard and garden was built for the family of cartographer and astronomer Cassini by Lemonnier, who followed Bélisard's blueprints. It is a two-story hôtel, with 11 axes, an elegant rotunda by the garden and considerable 18th and 19th century interior decoration. It has been a branch office of the Prime Minister since 1975.

122

Hôtel de La Vergne
1771-74
50, Rue de Vaugirard, 6e
Metro: St-Placide

This hôtel surrounds a courtyard, and was built between 1640 and 1650 for Isabelle Pena, wife of Marc Pioche de La Vergne. Its noble street portal was part of the renovations performed by the Duke of la Trémoïlle from 1771-74.

123

Hôtel de Crillon / Hôtel de Coislin
1775
Jacques-Ange Gabriel
10, Place de la Concorde, 8e
Metro: Concorde

The right hôtel, built on the northern side of the Place de la Concorde, was originally a royal storeroom (today for the Marine Ministry). The left complex was broken up into private residences. Both buildings are identical in design, with rococo adaptations of the Louvre colonnade, with rusticated rows of arches, 12 Corinthian columns, and a gabled corner forepart. The Hôtel de Crillon (owned after 1788 by the Duke of Crillon) was converted into a hotel after the Revolution.

124

Hôtel de Rochechouart
after 1776
Mathurin Cherpitel
110, Rue de Grenelle, 7e
Metro: Varenne

This house, built by Cherpitel for the Marquise of Courteille, presents an excellent example of the standard building style from the era of Louis XVI: elegant façade with colossal Corinthian pillars, buttress wings, and pilaster decor, all of which is mirrored in the interior. The plot was willed to the Marquis's daughter, the Comtesse de Rochechouart, and was acquired by the state in 1829. It has since been remodeled by various bureaucrats of the Education Ministry.

125

Théâtre de l'Odéon
1774 and 1780-82
Pierre Louis Moreau, Marie-Joseph Peyre, and
Charles de Wailly
Place de l'Odéon, 6e
Metro: Odéon

A replacement for the "Comédie Française" had been planned since 1767, and the king himself arranged for this land to be aquired from the Hôtel de Condé. Work began in 1774 under plans from Moreau, the city's chief architect, but the construction of this "Théâtre Français" was modified in 1780 to fit new designs by Peyre and Wailly. The result is a masterpiece of Classicism, with five secondary streets flowing in-to the semicircular plaza in front of the mono-lithic edifice, with its jointed rectangular blocks, colossal Doric portico, and its arcade entrance on the ground floor. The pyramidal roof and the arched links to the neighbouring buildings have been removed. The interior comprises a vestibule and a 4-story hall with 1,900 seats, revolutionary for its daring use of seats on the ground floor. The ceiling art was produced by André Masson in 1965. The building was twice renovated after fires, in 1799 and 1818.

126

Hôtel de Massa
1777-84
Jean-Baptiste Le Boursier
38, Rue du Faubourg-St-Jacques, 14e
Metro: Denfert-Rochereau

The hôtel, moved from the Champs-Elysées to the garden of the observatory in 1929, was originally built by Le Boursier for Thiroux de Montsauge, a financial clerk. This elegant, two-story square building boasts a jointed design and rows of reliefs above the ground-floor arcade. It was the seat of the Société des Gens des Lettres after 1838, and has been the seat of the Société Civile des Auteurs Multimédia since 1981.

127

La Bagatelle
1775
François Joseph Bélanger
Bois de Boulogne, 16e
Metro: Pont de Neuilly

This lovely castle in the park was the last surviving residence in Forêt de Rouvray, formerly a royal game preserve (the Longchamp abbey, founded 1260, and the Francois I's summer retreat Madrid were both destroyed during the Revolution). The castle was built at top speed to accommodate a bet between the Count of Artois (later Charles X) and his sister-in-law Marie Antoinette, with architect Bélanger helping him replace the original pavilion of Babiole of Marschall Victor d'Estrée. The original castle was small and dense (rectangular, with 3 axes and a rotunda by the garden), although more floors and a cupola were added by its British owners around 1835. The state forest (863 hectares) was converted by Adolphe Alphand after 1852 into a public park in honor of Napoleon III, including the Longchamp horse track in 1857, the Auteuil hippodrome in 1873, and a rose garden in 1905.

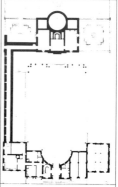

128

Hôtel Bourbon-Condé
after 1782
Alexandre Théodore Brongniart
12, Rue Monsieur, 7e
Metro: St. François-Xavier

Brongniart purchased this large parcel and resold it in pieces to those willing to engage him as their architect. Louis Joseph de Bourbon-Condé was among the buyers in 1780, and this elegant house between a yard and a garden, erected from 1782, was Brongniart's masterpiece, with a three-wing design, a low coachhouse, a bulging middle section by the scantly decorated garden, and Ionic pilasters (on the center forepart by the street).

129

Parc de Monceau
after 1778
Louis Carmontelle, Thomas Blaikie and Adolphe Alphand
35, Boulevard de Courcelles, 8e
Metro: Monceau

Styled after the modern English "Chinese Garden," Louis Philippe d'Orléans (then the Duke

of Chartres, later Philippe Egalité) commissioned Carmontelle, a writer, to create a park south of the Monceau village. This creation of 1778 was remodeled around 1783 by the Scottish landscaper Blaikie, whose famous park, "la folie de Chartres," took up only half the original space. The current form, covering 8.5 hectares, was established by Alphand in 1861. One of Claude Nicolas Ledoux's tollhouses, a rounded Doric temple between magnificent grills (design by Gabriel Davioud), sits on the northern side. Few garden structures remain, including the Egyptian pyramid, the obelisk of "Naumachie" (depicting a battle at sea) as a water fountain with a colonnade (taken from the remains of the Valois chapel from the St-Denis cathedral, which was torn up in 1719), and a Renaissance arcade from the city hall, which burned down in 1871.

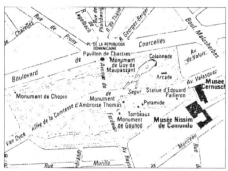

130

Barrière d'Enfer
1784-87
Claude Nicolas Ledoux
Place Denfert-Rochereau, 14e
Metro: Denfert-Rochereau

These two symmetrical square pavilions were built by Ledoux as tollhouses on the 24-kilometer long "mur murant Paris" for the Chief Tax Collector. Building #1 includes a way down into the "Catacombs," formerly a quarry, where the remains of over 6 million dead were transfered beginning in 1785 from excavated inner-city graveyards.

|3|
Hôtel de Salm
1782-88
Pierre Rousseau
64, Rue de Lille, 7e
Metro: Solférino

This elegant antique city mansion, built by Rousseau for the extravagant taste of Prince Fredrich III of Salm-Kyrburg, was built on land acquired in 1782. In 1804, it became the head-quarters of Napoleon's Légion d'Honneur, founded two years earlier. Until 1812, the palace was renovated by Marie-Joseph Peyre. Reconstruction by Anastase Motier continued for three more years after a fire in 1871. A triumph arch provides an entryway from the Rue de Lille into a forecourt with Ionic colonnades and a Corinthian portico. The low façade near the river (with a pre-vaulted rotunda with half columns, jointed intersections, gabled windows, and niches for busts) originally led into a garden terrace. Note the excellent Classical building sculpture from Jean-Guillaume Moitte and Philippe-Laurent Roland.

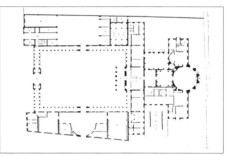

|32|
Hôtel de Galliffet
1784-91
François Etienne Legrand
73, Rue de Grenelle, 7e
Metro: Rue du Bac

This house, built for Simon de Galliffet, shows many of the architecture stylings of Louis XVI's era, with 9 axes, huge Ionic columns on the façade, in the rectangular salon, and in the rounded stairwell. The Italian Cultural Institute was established here in 1962.

133
Place de la Nation
1785-87
Claude Nicolas Ledoux
11e-12e
Metro: Nation

Until 1793, this plaza was called "Place du Trône," referring to a throne for Louis XIV on this ancient road to Vincennes. Between 1785-87, Ledoux added two tollhouses and two gigantic columns. After 1794, this newly renamed "Place du Trône-Renversé" was outfitted with a guillotine. Artist A.-J. Dalou was commissioned to create a fountain sculpture of "The Triumph of the Republic," eventually finished in 1899.

134
Théâtre-Français
1786-90
Victor Louis
Place Colette, 1er
Metro: Palais-Royal

To replace the Opera House (destroyed by fire in 1781), the Duke of Chartres commissioned Victor Louis to build this new, highly-modern, 2,000 seat box theater, including a metal roof, ceiling, and supports. The actors of the Comédie Française (founded in 1680) moved in ca. 1799 and began performances of Molière and Corneille. The current façade with the ground-floor colonnade dates back to 1863, when builder Prosper Chabrol built the entire Avenue de l'Opéra.

135
Rotonde de la Villette
1786-92
Claude Nicolas Ledoux
Place de Stalingrad, 19e
Metro: Gare d'Austerlitz

This masterpiece of "Revolutionary architecture" was Ledoux's centerpiece of the 54 customs houses of the "Enceinte des Fermiers Généraux," a 24-kilometer long wall around Paris. The massive stone quadrant with 4 identical porticos and a rotunda with Doric columns draws on a primordial monumentality and power. The building has housed the Commission du Vieux Paris since 1959.

136

Jardin des Plantes
1739-88
Georges L. Buffon
Place Valhubert, 5e

Metro: Jussieu

The park, built in 1626 as a medicinal root garden for Louis XIII's personal physician, has served
as the National Museum of Natural History since
1797. The park features a geometric French garden, an English cultivated garden, and a labyrinth
from 1630 with a metal pavilion. Noteworthy
buildings include: the Hôtel de Magny (1650); a
classical amphitheater (1788 by Edme Verniquet); two symmetric glass-and-iron greenhous-
es from Charles Rohault de Fleury (1834-36).

137

Rue des Colonnes
1797-98
Joseph Bénard
2e

Metro: Bourse

This short arcade street by Bénard is a paragon
of "Revolutionary architecture," featuring glyph
– and palmette – adorned arches over "Doric"
pillars and columns.

138

Rue de Rivoli
after 1802
Charles Percier and Pierre François Léonard Fontaine
1er

Metro: Palais-Royal

A union between the eastern and western axes
of Paris was already long planned when
Napoleon, then a consul, arranged for the sale
of some of the Republic's land, mostly on the
site of an old cloister. This particular section was
planned to be lined with unified ashlar façades.
The quietly refined arcade street includes many
businesses. A string of balconies, long since altered, ran along the second and fourth floors,
as well as the roof levels.

139

Hôtel de Beauharnais

1713-15 and after 1803
Germain Boffrand and Nicolas Bataille
78, Rue de Lille, 7e
Metro: Solférino

Built by Boffrand as an investment, and sold to Jean-Baptiste Colbert de Torcy, the house has been renovated numerous times. Eugène Rose de Beauharnais acquired the house in 1803 and subsequently arranged for Bataille to remodel luxuriously, including an Egyptian portico, an "Empire" room with Pompeian frescoes, and a Turkish boudoir. The hôtel was sold to Fredrich Wilhelm III, the King of Prussia, in 1818 and today houses the German Embassy.

140

Arc de Triomphe du Carrousel

1806-08
Charles Percier and Pierre François Léonard Fontaine
Place du Carrousel, 1er
Metro: Palais Royal

This triumph arch was built from 1806-08 in honour of Napoleon's victories. Although it today stands isolated, it was originally built as the entrance to the courtyard of the Tuileries castle. The design by Percier and Fontaine follows Roman models, including a quadriga of the Goddess of Victory (the original sculpture, of the Horses of San Marco, was returned to Venice). Napoleon designed the inscription himself.

141

Place du Châtelet

1802-10
1er-4e
Metro: Châtelet

This plaza is named for the Grand Châtelet, a 12th century bulwark which protected the islands of the Seine. Napoleon ordered the fortress demolished between 1802-10, replaced with the "Fontaine du Palmier," including Nicolas Bralle's victory pillar (1806-08). The plaza is flanked by two almost identical theaters: one is the Théâtre Sarah Bernardt, known as the Théâtre de la Ville since 1967, the other is the Operetta Theatre, since 1980 the Théâtre Musical de Paris.

142

Arc de Triomphe

1806-36
Jean François Thérèse Chalgrin
Place Charles de Gaulle
Metro: Charles de Gaulle-Etoile

This grandiose triumph arch (50 meters high and 45 meters wide) sits at the vertex of twelve streets, acting as a gigantic counterbalance to the Point-de-vue at the other end of the Champs-Elysées. Built on the site of two old customs houses by Ledoux (1785), the arch puts into practice the civil engineering theories of Baron Haussmann and the plaza designs of Jakob Ignaz Hittorff. The concepts for this imposing conclusion to the Champs-Elysées were researched between 1798 and 1802, and again in 1806; Napoleon commissioned Jean François Thérèse Chalgrin to build this monument to the glory of the French army. By 1809 the plans were finalized and the project begun, but work was broken off in 1814. Louis XVIII ordered it resumed in 1823, this time to immortalize the Victory of Bourbones in Spain. It was finished in 1836, and a Grave of the Unknown Soldier was added in 1921.

This massive, simple arch (open on the short sides) is without columnar formations or a quadriga. Its fine sculptural adornment builds harmoniously, with themes and artists chosen by Minister Adolphe Thiers in 1833. Selections include: "La Marseillaise/Revolt of the Free-Willed, 1792" by François Rude; "Napoleon's Triumph of 1810" by Jean-Pierre Cortot; and "Revolt of 1814" and "Peace of 1815" by Antoine Etex. Six reliefs of wartime battles are carved high in the vaulting of the arch, and a frieze of "Departure and Return of the French Army" is situated beneath the entablature. The names of victorious battles are inscribed on 30 signs on the attic. The arch was restored from 1988-90.

98

143

Exchange House
1808 and 1821-26
Alexandre Théodore Brongniart and Eloi E. de Labarre
Place de la Bourse, 2e

Metro: Bourse

Napoleon felt it important that the stock exchange (founded 1724) be housed in a new building which could adequately reflect the "grandeur of the capital." Brongniart began construction in 1808 on the site of St. Thomas, an old Domincan cloister; his design resembled a rectangular, single-story temple. The project was eventually completed by de Labarre from 1821-26. Later expansion by J.B. Cavel included a cruciform surrounded by innumerable columns (1902-05).

144

Stock Exchange
1767, 1809-13 and 1886-90
Nicolas Le Camus de Mézières, François Joseph Bélanger and Henri Blondel
2, Rue de Viarmes, 1er

Metro: Les Halles

The Hôtel de Soissons, built for Catherine de' Medici in 1571, was torn down in 1748 but several of the 31-meter-high Doric columns erected around 1575 by Jean Bullant remain. A rounded "Halle au Blé" by de Mézières was added in 1767. After a fire in 1802, a Revolutionary-style cast iron cupola was added between 1809 and 1813 by Bélanger. Blondel later glazed it as he converted the building into a stock exchange (1886-90).

145

Place de la Bastille
1831-40
Jean Antoine Alavoine
4e-11e-12e

Metro: Bastille

The Bastille, a rectangular fortress build by Charles V from 1370-82 to protect his Hôtel St-Paul, stood atop this wide plaza until 1789. Napoleon initiated construction of a fountain but this project later became the "Colonne de Juillet," a 50-meter high column monument with a spiral staircase in the middle of the plaza atop the graves of the victims of the July Revolution. Alavoine designed the column, engraved with the names of the 504 who died.

146

Hôtel de Pontalba

1876
Félix Langlois
41, Rue du Faubourg-St-Honoré, 8e
Metro: Concorde

This townhouse, originally built by Louis Visconti for the Marquise de Pontalba between 1836 and 1842, was rebuilt by Langlois for Baron Edmond de Rothschild in 1876 entirely in the style of the Louis XV era. The carriage house entrance conceals a second courtyard and the three-story *corps de logis*. The building was taken over by the American government in 1948 and has served as the American Embassy since 1966.

147

National Bank of Paris

1839
Victor Lemaire
20, Boulevard des Italiens, 9e
Metro: Opéra

This Restoration bank building, erected by Lemaire in 1839, served as the model for Marcel Proust's famous "Maison Dorée." Architect Pierre Dufau extended the square building and its delicate patterns to the Rue Taitbout in 1976.

148

Winter Circus

1852
Jakob Ignaz Hittorff
110, Rue Amelot, 11e
Metro: Filles du Calvaire

Napoleon commissioned Hittorff from Cologne to build this heated circus as a gift to the French citizens. The twenty-sided building held 6,000 visitors within its 48-meter diameter and 28-meter high confines. The richly colored exterior foundation is really a plinth supporting columns, which in turn bear the light roof. Decorations include amazons (by James Pradier) near the entrance, figured relief bars with scenes of mythological horses, a line of windows, and beams.

149

Ecole Nationale Supérieure des Beaux-Arts
1609 and after 1816
14, Rue Bonaparte, 6e
Metro: St-Germain-des-Prés

Marguerite de Valois, the first wife of Henri IV, acquired this land in 1603 to build a townhouse, although a small convent and its Chapel of Eternal Worship were built in 1609 for the Barefoot Augustiners. It was replaced in 1613 by the Petits-Augustins, who built a cloister from 1617-18. The rectangular church (Doric interior with a wooden barrel vault), its subsequent chapel (hexagonal with a wooden cupola dedicated to the sect's financial patron), and the simple cloister still remain, although the buildings were deconsecrated in 1790. A "Museum of French Monuments" was set up between 1791 and 1816, through which Alexandre Lenoir saved numerous souvenirs of the monarchy from the zealots of the Revolution. During that period, entire sections of the façades of the Gaillon castle (built between 1501 and 1511) and from Anet (1547-52) were brought to the courtyard. Several buildings were constructed to accommodate the art school which was founded here in 1816, including Francisque Joseph Duret's Bâtiment des Loges, whose artwork is modeled after Raphael's loggias. By 1836, part of the cloister had been converted into a Pompeian atrium by Félix Duban, and from 1841-42, Paul Delaroche painted his enormous "The Genius of Art Crowns Kings" in the lecture hall.

Duban would also redo the Palais des Etudes in a Renaissance style, including a library in its eastern part (1858-64).

The campus expanded in 1884 to the Hôtel de la Bazinière (de Chimay) on Quai Malaquais Nr. 17, with François Mansart rebuilding the mid-17th century, three-wing structure from 1653-1658.

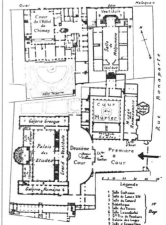

150
Ste-Geneviève Library
1844-50
Henri Labrouste
10, Place du Panthéon, 5e
Metro: Luxembourg

This library was built on the site of the Montaigu College, originally founded in 1314. Planned by Labrouste in 1839 and built during much of the next decade, it was intended to house the treasures of the neighbouring cloister. Its long ashlar blocks are assembled in a neo-Renaissance style, enclosing a slender, two-story reading room on the upper floor (80×70 meters, with 315 seats added to the original 400 in 1932). The arcade layout includes a plinth with a central entrance and a staircase, with the names of 810 authors carved above. The building took an important step in the use of iron in architecture: note the 18 light cast iron columns and ornamental trusses bearing the decoratively painted vaulting, with the books on the long walls. The library was opened in 1851 and restored from 1989-90.

151
Travellers Club / Hôtel Païva
1856-66
Pierre Manguin
25, Champs-Elysées, 8e
Metro: Franklin D. Roosevelt

This refined mansion with forecourt once accommodated famous soirees by the Marquise de Païva y Araujo, a courtesan. Built in a mixed Italian and French Renaissance style, it has retained its interior decorations, known to be among the finest (and costliest) of the Second Empire. It has been a Travellers Club since 1904.

152

Gare du Nord
1861-65
Jakob Ignaz Hittorff
Place Napoléon-III, 10e
Metro: Gare du Nord

Funds were allocated in 1857 to replace the old Embarcadère de Belgique with a new train station. The 180-meter-long Classical façade with double Ionic pillars and gabled façade spreads to the two-story wings and corner pavilions. Note the statues of nine European cites, as well as 12 northern French destinations. The station interior encompasses a wide hall of metal and glass (200×70 meters, with 2 rows of cast iron columns 38 meters in height).

153

Buttes-Chaumont Park
1864-67
Adolphe Alphand
Place Armand-Carrel, 19e
Metro: Buttes-Chaumont

This artistic park was built for Napoleon III on the site of a 13th century quarry. It includes a grotto, a waterfall, and even a mountain lake, atop which a round Corinthian temple sits 35 meters above the water (the design resembles the Vesta temple near Tivoli, by Gabriel Davioud, who also designed guardhouses and cafes). It has undergone renovations since 1977.

154

Maison "Opéra"
1867-68
Charles Garnier
5, Rue du Dr. Lancereaux, 8e
Metro: Miromesnil

This magnificent town house with a flat relief from the French Renaissance was built by the Marquis de Luzarches d'Azay. It is a symmetric building, with 3 pillared floors and roof lucarnes, although the rounded-arch portal is in a different style. Its interior rooms progress successively from Renaissance styles to the modes of Louis XVI.

155

Théâtre National de l'Opéra
1862-75
Charles Garnier
Place de l'Opéra, 9e
Metro: Opéra

After the old Opera House was temporarily closed in 1858, Napoleon III mulled ideas for a new building to replace it. The results left a telling monument to the nature of French culture during the Second Empire, as conceived by young Charles Garnier, who lead architect honours after a fierce competition in 1860. Ground was broken in 1862 as part of a program to renew the entire quarter. It was consecrated in 1875.

The magnificent, freestanding building is designed so that the different rooms—the foyer, staircase, stage, and auditorium with reserved space for nobility—can be identified from the outside. Combining architectonic motifs of Italian and French Mannerism and the Baroque era, the colorful façade is made of numerous materials and faces the Avenue de l'Opéra with freestanding steps, an arcade floor, a colonnade of double columns, side lofts, and an attic. It should not be missed that the forecourt, the opulently decorated staircase, and in particular the foyer with paintings by Paul Baudry announce that this opera, at its core, serves the self-image of its middle and upper class visitors. The sculptural adornment is almost overwhelming, coming from 73 different artists, including the risqué but famous "Dancers" by Jean-Baptiste Carpeaux. On the western side, a double ramp leads to the Emperor's entrance, and behind the stage (52×37×60 meters) sits the Foyer de Danse, decorated by Gustave C.R. Boulanger. Since the construction of the new Opéra de la Bastille (1989), this facility has contained only the Palais de la Danse.

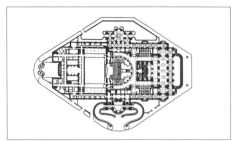

104

156
Hôtel de Ville
1873-82
Théodore Ballu and Pierre J.E. Deperthes
Place de l'Hôtel-de-Ville, 4e
Metro: Hôtel de Ville

Its predecessors were the "Maison des Piliers," a former city hall acquired by Etienne Marcel in 1357, and a newer building constructed by Domenico da Cortona, 1533-1628, around a courtyard. The central wing of the current complex, with extensions by E.H. Godde and J.B. Lesuer from 1837-49, corresponds roughly with that building; it was burned during the Commune Uprising. Ballu and Deperthes were commissioned to build a slightly modified copy of the original.

157
Fontaine des Quatre Parties du Monde
1874
Gabriel Davioud
Avenue de l'Observatoire, 6e
RER: Port-Royal

This magnificent neo-Baroque fountain by Davioud includes allegorical artwork about the continents (Jean-Baptiste Carpeaux), a globe with the zodiac (Eugène Legrain), and the animal world (Emmanuel Frémiet).

158
National Bank of Paris
1878-81
Edouard Jules Corroyer
14, Rue Bergère, 9e
Metro: Bonne-Nouvelle

A bombastic façade, adorned with feminine allegories, mosaics of the continents, and ships' prows, fronts this building with a mix of Renaissance and Baroque. The huge metal hall, topped with a mosaic frieze and ringed on three sides with columns that bear the ceiling, was contributed to this "Comptoir d'Escompte" by the Moisant company.

159

Eiffel Tower / Champ de Mars
1887-89
Gustave Eiffel
Quai Branly, 7e
Metro: Champ de Mars

This extended (35 hectares) grassy park dates back to 1765, when it was established as a training and parade field for up to 10,000 of the nearby Military Academy's men. It was converted into a horse racing track in 1780, next into fairgrounds for Revolution festivals, and in 1798 into an exhibition ground for industrial expositions. Although the greenery was reduced by Joseph Bouvard to 21 hectares between 1907 and 1927, a park was established and the pathways reconfigured; international shows were held here in 1867, 1878, 1889, 1900, and 1937, often featuring historically important glass-and-iron structures. Although constructions like Jean-Camille Formigé's "Palais des Beaux-Arts" and Ch.L. Ferdinand Dutert's splendid "Galerie des Machines" were torn down, one structure has not only remained intact, but has come to symbolize the city: the Eiffel Tower. Gustave Eiffel, who had been building metal bridges around the world for the twenty prior years, beat out 700 competitors to build a "Tower of 300 Meters."

The winning idea actually came from his colleagues, engineers Emile Nouguier and Maurice Koechlin, who suggested a concave skeleton of prefabricated steel (12,000 sections, 2,500,000 rivets) to allow the wind to pass through. Construction lasted only 16 months, as the nine-14 meter deep foundations for the 4 main pillars were laid 125 meters apart from each other.

The 7,000-ton tower resembles a slender pyramid and has three intermediary floors (at 57, 115, and 274 meters), accessible by stairs and elevators. The original construction was financed by a joint-stock company, and practical functions of the tower include an antenna, a light tower, a meteorological station, and a site for exhibits.

Historically, it will be remembered as the end of Historicism and the beginning of functional architectural design.

Restorations have been ongoing since 1983, including new illumination devices in 1986.

160

Théâtre de l'Opéra-Comique

1893-98

Stanislas Louis Bernier

Place Boieldieu, 2e

Metro: 4 Septembre

This massive neo-Baroque structure by Bernier is actually the third theater on this spot, after fires in 1838 and 1887. Renovations of the delightful interior with statues and wall-art lasted until 1989.

161

Maison Le Bihan / formerly Magasin Wimphen

1893-94

Charles de Montalto

25, Rue du Faubourg St-Antoine, 11e

Metro: Ledru-Rollin

The exterior of this combination business, fashion workshop, and residence explains its function clearly: ashlar and historic cast iron scaffolding frame the fully glass lower floor, while a private house sits above.

162

Ecole du Sacré-Cœur

1895

Hector Guimard

11, Avenue de La Frillière, 16e

Metro: Porte de St-Cloud

This three-story schoolhouse was built by Guimard for the priests of Sacré-Cœur. The groundfloor was once open, with v-shaped cast iron supports built after an 1855 drawing by Viollet-le-Duc for "Entretiens." Note the fine ornamental details and materials (including color bricks). The six lower rooms are naturally lit by group windows, conceptualized by Joseph Vaudremer and J. Baudot. It was converted into a residence with a subterranean garage in the courtyard in 1983.

163

Grand Palais
1897-1900
Charles Girault, Henri Deglane, Albert Thomas,
and Albert Louvet
Avenue Winston Churchill, 8e
Metro: Champs-Elysées-Clemenceau

This building, along with the Pont Alexandre III
and the Petit-Palais, comprise the peak of Belle
Epoque architecture. The neo-Baroque complex was built in 3 years for the International Exposition of 1900 by Girault, Deglane, Thomas,
and Louvet, co-winners of a competition. The
huge, historic stone façade – columnar front, a
frieze of enameled tiles entitled "The March of
Art through the Epochs," and striking quadrigas
by Georges Récipon – hides a magnificent
(45×192 meters) and bright hall of glass and
iron with continuous galleries. Art exhibitions
have been held here since 1971.

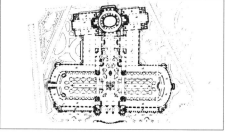

164

Petit-Palais
1897-1900
Charles Girault
Avenue Winston Churchill, 8e
Metro: Champs-Elysées-Clemenceau

The "Little Palace," an exhibition house imitating
18th-century styles, contained a retrospective of
French art. It featured powerful Ionic colonnades
with corner pavilions and a domed middle,
rich sculptural adornment, excellent metalwork,
freestanding steps, a vestibule, and galleries
around a yard. The house has been fittingly used
as the "Musée du Petit-Palais."

165

Pont Alexandre III
1896-1900
Jean Résal, Amédé Alby, Cassien Bernard, and Gaston Cousin
7e-8e
Metro: Champs-Elysées-Clemenceau

This most impressive bridge was built as a symbol of the Russian-French alliance of 1892. Ground was broken in 1896 by Czar Nicholas II, with the plans by the team of engineers. Note the metal segmented arch (109 meters long, 40 meters wide) and the pylons acting as supports, as well as the extensive sculpturing from Emmanuel Frémiet and Aimé-Jules Dalou.

166

Musée d'Orsay
1898-1900
Victor Laloux
9, Quai Anatole-France, 7e
Metro: Solférino

Architect Laloux won a competition for the commission of designing a magnificent train station with a hotel for the Orléans train line, all on the former site of the Palais d'Orsay (destroyed in 1871). The glass and metal construction of the broad halls (40×140 meters) distracts the richly-sculptured stone walls. The Gare d'Orsay was largely unusable by 1937, and in 1971 it was nearly destroyed in favor of a 1,000-bed hotel. Instead, the decision was made in 1977 to replace it with a museum for art of the period between 1848-1914. The main hall was reconfigured between 1983-86 by the "ACT-architecture" group (Pierre Colboc, René Bardon and Jean-Paul Philippon). The interior decor was planned anew by Italian architect Gae Aulenti.

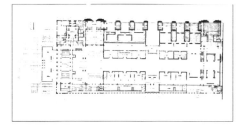

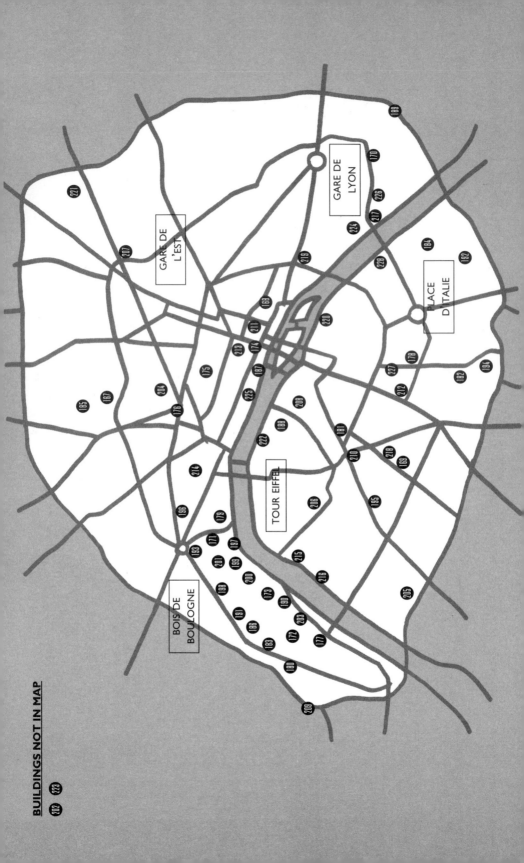

BUILDINGS NOT IN MAP

202 223

GARE DE LYON

GARE DE L'EST

PLACE D'ITALIE

TOUR EIFFEL

BOIS DE BOULOGNE

Religious and Secular Buildings from Art Nouveau to the Present

Turn-of-the-century style replaced the historical forms of the 19th century with organic ornamentation and introduced Modernism into Parisian architecture. Hector Guimard's subway entrances become synonymous with Art Nouveau, which itself in turn became known as the "style métro." Perret's first reinforced concrete towers broke even fresher ground. His ideas about execution and use, as well as standardizing and industrializing concrete construction, were particularly influential to Le Corbusier, whose strongly geometric "Studio-houses" emerged from experimentation with the possibilities and aesthetics of concrete.

1950 saw a new development in Parisian architecture: the construction of the La Défense district in the western part of the city. Its 26 high-rises forever altered the traditional view from the Louvre along the Champs-Élysées, accentuating new silhouettes to the city skyline. The Boulevard Périphérique of 1971 circled the inner city, separating it from the numerous satellite cities, which themselves were subjected to a tremendous growth in construction. Finally, with François Mitterrand's "Grands Projets," the last decade has brought the fresh air of new accents to the center of old Paris.

167

St-Jean-l'Evangeliste
1894-1904
Anatole de Baudot
19, Rue des Abbesses, 18e
Metro: Abbesses

This church, built by Baudot and consecrated by Johannes the Evangelist, is an early example of iron-and-concrete architecture (the System Cottancin). A three-aisle room (22×44 meters) sits above the crypts, featuring varied bay designs, continuous heights, 26 rectangular supports, and "Gothic" ribbed vaulting (7 cm thick, flat above the aisles, rising to a dome in the central elevation). The façade is slender, with red bricks and staircase towers; the green ceramic bands—including the busts of Johannes and 2 angels on the doors—are from Alexandre Bigot.

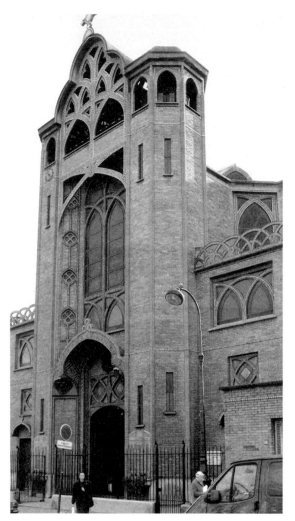

168

Synagogue
1913
Hector Guimard
10, Rue Pavée, 4e
Metro: St-Paul

This synagogue was built for a Russian-Polish Jewish group in 1913 and was consecrated a year later. Highlights include a small, inlaid, re-inforced concrete rectangle on the wavy façade (with small windows), the Two Tablets on the gable, a bright, white-painted, three-aisle room with two upper floors and overhead lighting. The original decorations with gold-accentuated ornamentation remain.

169

Notre-Dame-du-Travail
1899-1900
Jules Astruc
59, Rue Vercingétorix, 14e
Metro: Pernéty

This exceptional, inexpensive building sits in a blue-collar quarter and replaced the Notre-Dame-de-Plaisance parish church. Materials for the pseudo-Roman ashlar exterior and the highly-modern metal interior came from the International Exposition of 1900. The bright, three-aisle church (47×28 meters) with flanking chapels beneath elevations resembles rolled-iron work halls that have been riveted together. Half-timber binders link the thin supports and the metal roof.

170

Saint-Esprit
1928-35
Paul Tournon
186, Avenue Daumesnil, 12e
Metro: Daumesnil

This memorial church was built in the vicinity of the Colonial Exposition of 1931 for Catholic missionaries. It is a revealing paraphrase of the Hagia Sophia, with a massive (85-meter high) concrete entrance tower with red brick lining and a fabulous ring of lights beneath the cupola (33 meters high, 23-meter diameter).

171

St-Pierre-de-Chaillot
1931-38
Emile Bois
35, Avenue Marceau, 16e
Metro: George V

This Romanic-Byzantinian concrete church was built by Emile Bois, winner of an architectural contest (1926). It includes a massive ashlar façade with side towers, and a sub-and super-church in the form of a Greek cross, with five eight-sided domes, the middle of which is 46 meters high.

172
Castel Béranger
1897-98
Hector Guimard
14, Rue La Fontaine, 16e
Metro: Jasmin

Guimard built this most famous of his apartment complexes for the Fournier widow according to his plans of 1895. It merited an award by the city in 1899. The six-story corner house, which surrounds a courtyard on three sides, distinguishes itself primarily through a constant variation of materials (ashlar, brick, ceramic, and cast iron), detail forms (size and shapes of windows, layouts of apartments), and the rich plant (on the door columns), animal (roof and balcony), and abstract (door column) ornamentation. The 36 apartments offer bright rooms outfitted with full bath and telephones, oriented for middle-class tenants. Outfitted from wallpaper to the faucets by Guimard himself, many of the minute ornaments remain.

Several other of Guimard's apartment buildings are in the vicinity: #17-21 Rue La Fontaine (1909-11); #11 Rue François-Millet (1910); and the Hôtel Mezzara (#60 Rue La Fontaine, 1910-11) for Paul Mezzara, a painter and textile industrialist.

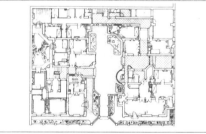

173
Residential Building
1903
Auguste Perret
25bis, Rue Benjamin-Franklin, 16e
Metro: Trocadéro

This early example of a concrete residence hall was built by Perret to be managed by him. It includes a steep building without a yard, a business in the ground floor, nine stories for apartments, two side projections, and a cornered, retreating middle (designed to improve the lighting) on the top three floors. Even if hidden by panels and filled plant sculptures of Bigot ceramic, the concrete framework allows for the large windows.

174

Metro Stations
1895-96 and 1900
Plans for the subway (Métropolitain) were begun in 1855, although the work did not commence until 1895. The first 8 stations on Line 1, stretching over the 10 kilometers from Porte de Vincennes to Porte Maillot, opened on 17 July, 1900, three months after the beginning of the International Exposition. Although a design competition was held in 1899, the President did not give the commission to any of the prize winners, instead favoring Hector Guimard to design the entrances to the Metro. His cast-iron-and-glass entrances, famously painted green, have almost all been removed, although a few beautiful examples remain at Porte Dauphine (16e) and Place des Abbesses (18e). The design styles varied greatly to include bright, inscribed and framed entrances, sheltered entrances, and complete stations with windows. With their floral forms – the lamps resemble long-stemmed flowers – these stations personify the Art Nouveau fundaments of the Style Métro.

175

Office Building (Le Parisien Libéré)
1904-05
Georges Chédanne
124, Rue Réaumur, 2e
Metro: Sentier
This unusual house features a plainly visible framework of brown-painted metal, window frames from narrowly divided panes, and three-sided balconies on the fourth floor. The bright stories include highly divisible planes and highly resilient floors. Only the fifth floor boasts brickwork, with portals decorated in Art Nouveau motifs. Note the branching of the lode-bearing iron supports on the ground floor. This building housed the "Parisien Libéré" newspaper from 1944-73.

176

Lafayette Department Store

1906-08 and 1910-12
Georges Chédanne and F. Chanut
40, Boulevard Haussmann, 9e
Metro: Chaussée d'Antin

This department store, founded by Théophile Bader and Alphonse Kahn in 1894, has grown steadily. From 1906-12, Chanut oversaw the addition of concrete wings. Air conditioning, electric lighting, and an Art Déco façade of granite were added during renovations in 1926. Only one of the 2 original 23-meter high central rooms (Art Nouveau decor, with multiple-story galleries with metal bars and a colorful glass dome as the light source) survived the renovations of 1958.

177

Hôtel Guimard

1909-10
Hector Guimard
122, Avenue Mozart, 16e
Metro: Jasmin

This relatively small (90 square meters) private residence was built by Guimard after his marriage to the American painter Adeline Oppenheim. It is a refined building, with a three sided plot. The rooms follow each other in widely varied ways among its 4 floors. The asymmetrical façade is made of ashlar, brick, and cast iron bars. Across the way sits the Villa Flore, built by Guimard between 1924 and 1926, a smooth brick building reminiscent of Art Nouveau styles.

178

Workshop

1911-12
André Arfvidson
31, Rue Campagne-Première, 14e
Metro: Raspail

This ingenious façade was created by Arfvidson out of Alexandre Bigot's colorful ceramic. Large workshops and two-story apartments sit behind the concrete and metal frames.

179

Théâtre des Champs-Elysées
1911-13
Auguste Perret
13-15, Avenue Montaigne, 8e
Metro: Alma-Marceau

The first designs were drafted by Henri Van de Velde, who called in Perret to build a concrete scaffolding because of the poor terrain but was supplanted by him as architect and employer. Veined marble siding covers the high, pillar-like, rectangular, framed façade, with strongly advancing horizontal roofs, sober Classical outlines, and a concrete skeleton with fanned-out bricks. The bare interior is cleverly divided through unconcealed concrete supports (25 meters high).

180

Hôtel Guadet
1912
Paul Guadet
25, Boulevard Murat, 16e
Metro: Porte d'Auteuil

This notable house, built for himself by artist Paul Gaudet, an "apostle" of the concrete movement, is made of concrete with yellow-brown mosaic tile decor. It includes a concrete skeleton with 6 axes, three stories, large windows, two balconies, and a flat roof—all models for Gaudet's student Auguste Perret. The building was extended in 1924 to the Rue du Général Delestraint.

181

Terrace House
1912-13
Henri Sauvage
26, Rue Vavin, 6e
Metro: Vavin

This early terrace house (Maison à gradins), with one terrace per apartment, is covered with bluish-white tiles. It is T-shaped and seven stories high, although it only begins sloping inward after the third floor. Built in the "cité-Jardin verticale" style, it demonstrates a considerable to Viennese influence.

182

Ozenfant Workshop
1922-23
Le Corbusier and Pierre Jeanneret
53, Avenue Reille, 14e
Metro: Porte d'Orléans

Le Corbusier and his cousin Pierre Jeanneret built this almost perfectly preserved Purist masterpiece for a friend, the fashion artist, painter, and theorist Amédée Ozenfant. The four-story concrete corner house sits on an irregular plot, and includes a ground-floor apartment (originally a garage) and a concrete spiral which originally served as the entrance to the second floor and which itself has rows of windows and artists' workshops with huge corner windows.

183

Laroche and Jeanneret Villas
1923-25
Le Corbusier
8-10, Square du Docteur-Blanche, 16e
Metro: Jasmin

Although he had initially sought to employ funding by the Banque Immobilière de France to create an entire street of exclusive residences, stringent construction stipulations allowed Le Corbusier to complete only two of these single-family houses: one for his musician brother Albert and another for his friend Raoul Laroche, a Swiss banker. The stark Villa Jeanneret is linked to the Villa Laroche on its small side. The interior was clearly created according to the owner's desires: the sociable young Laroche had owned an impressive collection of modern art. The high halls create a sort of "promenade d'architecture," with a succession of straight polychromatic cubes, terraces, transparent vantage points, and ramps. Because Albert had several children, his brother included multiple small rooms for them in the design. Both houses have been in the possession of the "Fondation Le Corbusier" since 1968.

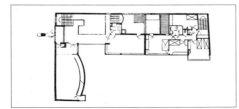

184
Villa Planeix
1924-28
Le Corbusier and Pierre Jeanneret
24bis, Boulevard Masséna, 13e
Metro: Porte d'Ivry

This cubist house was built for the gravestone carver Antonin Planeix. It is made of white concrete blocks atop a glassy base. The play between openings and projections on the flat planes exhibits a subtle touch. Note the banks of windows on the bedrooms, the balcony above the square projections denoting the workshops, and the terrace in front of the roof floor. An open façade with steep steps leads to the minuscule garden in the back.

185
Maison Tristan Tzara
1922-30
Adolf Loos
15, Avenue Junot, 18e
Metro: Lamarck-Caulaincourt

This residence is the only work from Viennese architect Adolf Loos from his time in Paris (1922-1930). It was planned for the dada poet Tristan Tzara (1896-1963) in 1925 and executed over the next four years. Its form resembles two square blocks laid atop one another; the lower block is thick and unpainted, with two openings leading into the service area, a garage to the left, and a recessed rental apartment with a balcony niche. The upper block with the owner's rooms is painted white, with three symmetrical windows, a deep balcony, and a terraced roof over a complex chain of three floors of differently sized rooms around the salon and dining room. The higher side contains the garden and is terraced.

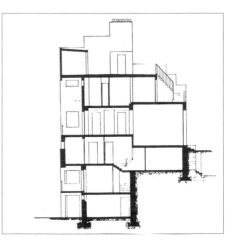

186

Rue Mallet-Stevens
1926-27
Robert Mallet-Stevens
Rue Mallet-Stevens, 16e
Metro: Ranelagh

Mallet-Stevens designed the unique ensemble of individual villas that make up this street. He planned the six houses and watchhouse for rich city dwellers, including himself (9, Rue Docteur-Blanche) and his friends (builders Joel and Jan Martel, among others). Each house is comprised of smooth white cubes with sharply-cut window frames and hard projections and depressions following the architectural principal: "L'architecte sculpte un énorme bloc, la maison."

187

"Samaritaine" Department Store
1928-30
Frantz Jourdain and Henri Sauvage
10-14, Quai du Louvre, 1er
Metro: Pont Neuf

Planning for the expansion of this premier department store (founded by Ernest Cognacq) to the Seine began in 1925, although the store had been stretching itself out since 1869. Jourdain, in the store's service beginning 1883, teamed up with Sauvage to petition against the prefect to overturn his ban against colorful metal buildings with domes along the river. They were allowed to construct a vertical stone façade with Art Déco motifs, which covers up a quickly-erected steel scaffolding.

188

"Maison de Verre"
1928-32
Pierre Chareau and Bernard Bijvoet
31, Rue St-Guillaume, 7e
Metro: Rue du Bac

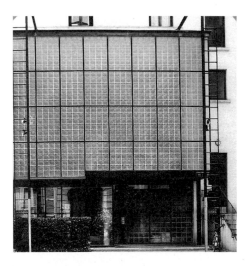

This functional house was built for Dr. Jean Dalsace, a gynecologist. His office is on the ground floor, the reception room is on the first floor, and the second story and the additional wing contain private rooms. The stone roof floor also dates from the original building, to which a metal scaffold was added. It is fully glassed on both sides, the inner dividers are fully movable and the ceiling can be rotated. The decorations are prototypical of Le Corbusier's "machinisme" style.

189

Musée des Arts Africains et Océaniens
1928-31
Léon Jaussely and Albert Laprade
293, Avenue Daumesnil, 12e
Metro: Porte Dorée

This museum, built upon the urging of Marschall Lyautey, was an influential exhibition of the French Empire, accompanying the Colonial Exposition of 1931. It was rebuilt and re-developed at the end of that display by André Malraux, who in 1960 envisioned its current concept: a neo-Classical concrete rectangle with granite covering (88×66 meters), high plinths, freestanding steeps, and a 14-meter high "colonnade" of square Ionic pillars.

190

Perret Workshop
1929-32
Auguste Perret
51-55, Rue Raynouard, 16e
Metro: Passy, Ranelagh

This building was a late work of concrete pioneer Perret and his workshop, with a visible reinforced iron frame, cast stone filling, and vertical windows. The house takes excellent advantage of a difficult plot, and composes its apartments around a circular salon. A magnificent spiral staircase leads to the offices through the passageway (with glass walls) to the Rue Berton. Perret lived in the top two floors.

191

Crédit Lyonnais
1930-31
J. Charavel and M. Melendes
65, Rue Saint-Didier / Rue des Belles-Feuilles, 16e
Metro: Victor Hugo

This admirable corner building by J. Charavel and M. Melendes houses an apartment building and a movie house (the Cinéma Victor Hugo). Its rounded tower on concrete supports features a rounded chain of balconies on its long sides.

192

Cité de Refuge de l'Armée du Salut
1929-33
Le Corbusier and Pierre Jeanneret
12, Rue Cantagrel, 13e

Metro: Porte d'Ivry

This gigantic ten-story Salvation Army building on a narrow, small, downward-sloping plot was funded by music patron Winaretta Singer, the Princess of Polignac. She commissioned Le Corbusier for the project, who began with the help of his cousin Pierre Jeanneret in 1929. The "Usine du Bien" serves as a nightly haven for 500, a canteen, and a center for reeducation. Architecturally, it demonstrates Le Corbusiers's theories about light, ventilation, and communal living in the city of the future–all early forms of the "Unité d'Habitation." The southern façade of this richly glassy, screened main building–a curtained façade with a metal scaffold–needed many changes. Sliding windows were added to the house in 1935–it initially was ventilated only by air conditioning–and sun blinds were added in 1952. The red-yellow-blue color scheme was added in 1975. The glass-bricks on the rear side were added by the Saint-Gobain firm. The entryway is comprised of displayed geometric forms, acting as a bridge between cubes and cylinders.

193

Residential Building
1933
Le Corbusier and Pierre Jeanneret
24, Rue Nungesser-et-Coli, 16e

Metro: Michel-Ange-Molitor

Framed in the Revolutionary style, this building is comprised of 8 fully-glassed stories, the uppermost terraced inwards. It features sliding windows and glass bricks and a black iron framework. The floors are of variable sizes – making it a predecessor of countless high-rise apartment buildings – and Le Corbusier made the 7th and 8th floors his private residence. A garden sits on the roof. Compare with #22 Rue Nungesser-et-Coli, a contemporary building by Michel Roux-Spitz.

194

Fondation Suisse / Cité Internationale Universitaire
1930-33
Le Corbusier and Pierre Jeanneret
7, Boulevard Jourdan, 14e
RER: Cité Universitaire

First suggested in 1920 by minister André Honnorat and built with the aid of grants, this international student community was built on 40 hectares of land that once held old city fortifications. It is comprised of 37 pavilions, built between 1923 and 1968, the most famous of which is the Swiss pavilion, built by Le Corbusier and his cousin Pierre Jeanneret from 1930-33 despite many obstacles. It includes

50 standardized rooms for students, a dining room, a library, office space, an apartment for the director, and a lodge for the concierge. The sound-proofed building, perched atop 19-meter high concrete posts, realizes the famous "5 points d'architecture nouvelle," according to which the Swiss hoped to renew urban construction: freestanding concrete supports (pilotis) on the open ground floor; a self-supporting metal scaffolding; a more free design, with side-by-side rooms along a 50-meter long corridor; a south façade acting as a freestanding curtained wall with window bank; and a rooftop garden. Unfortunately, its echo of the contemporary trend towards unadorned masterpieces was disastrous. Le Corbusier and Lucio Costa to also built the Fondation Franco-Brésilienne to from 1954-59.

195

Barillet Workshop
1931-32
Robert Mallet-Stevens
15, Square Vergennes, 15e
Metro: Vaugirard

This oft-overlooked workshop was built by Mallet-Stevens for the glass-artist Louis Barillet. It is a concrete rectangle with continuous banks of glass, with entry axes on the sides and a pre-vaulted office section with window banks. The three workshop floors are self-supporting, a terrace sits in front of the living rooms, and the roof is flat. The ground floor originally featured an entrance to the mosaic building, although it lacks an external elevator. It now houses architectural offices.

196

Former Shell Building
1932
L. Bechmann and L. Chatenay
45, Rue d'Artois / Rue Washington, 8e
Metro: St-Philippe-du-Roule

This 60,000-square-meter office, the largest of its time, was intended for 1,500 workers. Made dynamic through powerful buttresses, it is filled with cell-like double-windowed compartments. Using then-modern construction techniques, it was erected in only 20 months. Innovations included heating through radiators in the ceilings, central ventilation, and automatic elevators.

197

The City of Paris Museum of Modern Art
1934-37
Jean-Claude Dondel
11, Avenue du Président-Wilson, 16e
Metro: Iéna

This neo-Classical building was built for the 1937 World Exposition by Dondel, Viard, Aubert and Dastugue, winners of a design competition of 1934. The open forecourt with water basins faces the river, with single-story side wings, freestanding steps to the "cour d'honneur" with a steep colonnade. The main building is a concrete frame building with brick fanning beneath stone and marble platters.

198

Caserne des Sapeurs-pompiers
1935-36
Robert Mallet-Stevens
8, Rue Mesnil, 16e
Metro: Victor Hugo

This concrete building by Robert Mallet-Stevens serves both a functional and symbolic purpose. It contains a truck hall towards the courtyard, with a watchtower and control center above. The relaxation area and terrace are followed by a tower structure, a half-cylinder near the four stories of living quarters for 22 firefighters.

199

Economic and Social Council / Former Musée des Travaux Publics
1937
Auguste Perret
1, Avenue d'Iéna, 16e
Metro: Iéna

Perret designed this building for the Exposition des Arts et Techniques (1937). Part of the museum ensemble on the Chaillot hill, it was to be three wings around an interior yard and an entrance rotunda. Molded, fluted Egyptian columns adorn the southern wing, although the northern wing was only completed in 1962 and the eastern wing has never been built. The attic above the entranceway illuminates the conference room.

200

Palais de Chaillot
1937
Jacques Carlu, Léon Azéma, and Louis H. Boileau
Place du Trocadéro, 16e
Metro: Trocadéro

Plans were begun in 1811 for a mighty castle for the King of Rome (the son of Napoleon), and different plans of 1878 (by Gabriel Davioud, for the World Exposition) envisioned an awe-striking neo-Byzantine Palais du Trocadéro, with a colonnated rotunda, pavilions, and towers. The modern palace was built for the Exposition des Arts et Techniques of 1937, although it today holds the Marine Museum, Museum of Man, and Museum of French Monuments.

201

Fédération Nationale du Bâtiment
1949-51
Jean Prouvé
7, Rue La Pérouse, 16e
Metro: Kléber

This first Paris building with a curtained façade was built according to plans by Raymond Gravereaux and Raymond Lopez, although Prouvé handled the façade. It includes 8 levels divided into 14 sections, including a fully-glassed ground floor with 8 concrete supports, a yard with a subterranean lecture hall and water basins, and changeable office floors. The façade consists of 92-kilogram individual slates and folding plates, all within an aluminum frame attached to the concrete roof.

202

La Défense
after 1956

Metro: Neuilly-Défense

Named for the bronze "Défense de Paris" monument, this city district, ranked as the largest Paris construction project undertaken outside the confines of the Boulevard Périphérique (completed in 1973). Many designs were drawn up to widen the Louvre-Arc de Triomphe-Pont de Neuilly axis, beginning with a design competition of 1931. More realistic plans for a gigantic office district were drawn up in 1950 by Robert Camelot, Jean de Mailly, and Bernard Zehrfuss; construction began in 1956 with the CNIT (Centre Nationale des Industries et Techniques) exhibition hall. The result, finished in 1958, is a masterpiece of vaulting artistry on a triangular plot: three corner points—linked through steel cables spanning 230 meters—create the largest vaulting in the world.

The two-layered (6-cm thick) concrete sail by Nicolas Esquillan covers 100,000 square meters, and three aluminum façades were built by Jean Prouvé. A series of 30 high-rises built along a multi-story, 1,200-meter-long pedestrian zone were modeled in 1964. The offices were to have been built over a period of 30 years on 760 hectares of land. The high-rises, modeled primarily on American projects, emerged in three generations: between 1957 and 1963, J. and P. Greber and M.-L. Douglas built the Immeuble Esso, which, like all pre-1964 buildings, did not rise higher than 100 meters. The Tour Noble (built from 1964-66, by Jean de Mailly and Jacques Depussé, with Jean Prouvé) stretched to 32 floors with 25,000 square meters of floor space for 1,300 employees. The second generation of buildings included the 214-meter high Tour Gan, with 46 floors for 3,500 employees, built from 1972-74 by Jean Pierre Bisseuil as a steel structure around a concrete core, with the layout of a Greek cross. The Tour Assur (finished in 1974) by Pierre Dufau, Jean Pierre Dagbert, and Michel Stenzel is a star-shaped aluminum and tinted glass behemoth, reaching 230 meters in height, with 49 floors for 3,500 employees. The Tour Fiat, rising like a dark pillar to 230 meters in height, with 44 floors for 4,000 workers in large office spaces, was also finished in 1974 by Roger Saubot and François Jullien with Skidmore, Owings and Merrill. Michel Herbert and Michel Proux's Tour Manhattan, finished in 1975, deviated from the uniform rectangular forms and took the shape of two towers linked by a curved middle area. It is 100 meters high, with space for 2,900 employees in 28 floors of large office areas. The third stage began with the Tour Elf (by Saubot and Jullien, finished in 1985), conceptualized as a response to the oil crisis. Its improved climate controls and natural lighting—including individual windows for even the smallest offices—were intended to reduce energy costs. To accommodate this, the exterior surface needed to be enlarged and the main section of the building was divided into three parts. The final building was 180 meters high, with 48 stories for 4,000 employees.

203

Radio-France Headquarters
1952-63
Henri Bernard
116, Avenue du Président-Kennedy, 16e
Metro: Ranelagh, Passy, Mirabeau

This ring-like building has a reinforced concrete structure and atop 756 supports which make up for the uneven terrain. The outer ring (175-meter diameter, up to 37 meters high) features a curtained wall of aluminum and glass. The middle ring (10.5 meters high) houses the production departments, while the inner ring handles the signal dispatch, as well as a 70-meter high tower for archives. Climate control is provided through a dedicated warm-water spa (550 meters deep).

204

Office Building
1956-58
Jean Balladur and Benjamin Lebeigle
37, Rue de la Victoire, 9e
Metro: Le Peletier, Notre-Dame-de-Lorette

This building, erected as a Caisse Centrale de Réassurance, gamely attempts to bring a street corner to life by placing the slanted, rounded glass front of an office building up on concrete supports towards the street. It also represents the first attempt in Paris to create a curtained wall and a pure steel scaffold without inner supports, allowing for the completely free division of the rooms. Each individual section is proportioned according to Le Corbusier's "Modulor."

205

Palais des Sports
1959
Pierre Dufau and Victor Pajardis de Larivière
34, Boulevard Victor, 15e
Metro: Boulevard Victor

This is the successor of the famous "Vel d'Hiv," a bicycle racetrack from 1910. It was built on this irregular plot in just 6 months in 1959 by the Eiffel Establishment. The "geodetic dome" technique, developed by Richard Buckminster Fuller in 1952, was suggested by Pajardis after a research trip in America. 1,180 gleaming aluminum plates sitting between metal tube frames are organized into 6-part stars. The self-supporting dome sits above a circle with a 60-meter diameter.

206

UNESCO

1955-58

Marcel Breuer, Pier Luigi Nervi, and Bernard Zehrfuss

7, Place de Fontenoy, 7e

Metro: Ségur

With funding from all the member states, three architects—American Marcel Breuer, Italian Pier Luigi Nervi, and Frenchman Bernard Zehrfuss— were commissioned to build a headquarters for UNESCO, founded in 1945 in London. The complex is comprised of three buildings. The Secretariat came first, with 7 screened floors (1,068 windows on 72 V-shaped pilotis), a closed off front, a flat roof, over 800 rooms, and a grand portal with 2 layered canopies towards the garden, all on a Y-shaped plot with precarious sides. The conference building, a trapezoidal hall with a 70-meter span on 6 pillars with "fluted" concrete walls and an accordion-style roof, emerged next. Finally, the permanent delegations were served by a cubic building on the edge of a sheltering Japanese garden by Isamu Noguchi. Numerous works from famous artists adorned the buildings and open areas. Zehrfuss added subterranean additions with light wells in 1965.

207

French Communist Party Headquarters

1965-71

Oscar Niemeyer

2, Place du Colonel Fabien, 19e

Metro: Colonel Fabien

This was a late work of the Brazilian Oscar Niemeyer (with colleagues P. Chemetov, J. Deroche, J. Prouvé). The gently-rising, flat-laid forecourt is covered by a glass dome (1980) which serves as the light source for the subterranean meeting hall. The main structure is a curved, drawn-out glass rectangle on five concrete supports, with unmistakable traces of the architect's touch. Niemeyer also created the sculptures in front of the building.

208

Maisons des Sciences de l'Homme
1967-70
Marcel Lods, Henri Beauclair and Paul Depondt
54-56, Boulevard Raspail, 6e
Metro: Sèvres

This international contact center for researchers of all disciplines was erected on the former site of a jail. The two blocks include 10 and 5 fully-glassed floors respectively, with a visible steel scaffold (although no curtained wall), a concrete ceiling, and sound- and heat-proofing.

209

Parc-des-Princes Stadium
1969-72
Roger Taillibert
24, Avenue du Commandant-Guilbaud, 16e
Metro: Porte de St-Cloud, Exelmans

This functionalist building was created by Taillibert from prefabricated pieces. The oval, visible-concrete building of variable height sits atop 50 disc-shaped supports, which also hold up the 48-meter wide, overlapping roofing.

210

Montparnasse Tower
1969-73
Eugène Baudoin, Urbain Cassan, Louis de Hoyn de Marien, and Jean Saubat
33, Avenue du Maine, 15e
Metro: Montparnasse-Bienvenue

This 210-meter high office tower in front of the train station covers a 62×39 meters base and features a reinforced steel skeleton 58 floors high with glassed curtained walls. The building's statistics are impressive: 70-meter deep fundaments; 120,000 tons held up by 56 supports; 12-13,000 offices with 7,200 windows, and a 39,000 square meter surface area.

211

Centre National d'Art et de Culture Georges Pompidou
1972-77
Renzo Piano and Richard Rogers
Plateau Beaubourg, 4e
Metro: Rambuteau

Georges Pompidou's 1969 decision to proceed with this gigantic building led to a design competition in 1971 – won by designers Renzo Piano and Richard Rogers and engineer Ove Arup – and the eventual construction, which lasted from 1972-77. The result is a sunken, six-story, fully-glassed steel building with varied floor plans (150×150 meters), exterior escalators, and colorfully-painted exterior plumbing. The 42-meter high rectangle is held together through 14 steel pipes linked at "gerberettes" (junctions). The building houses the "Musée national d'art moderne," the "Centre de Création Industrielle," the "Bibliothèque Publique d'Information," and other institutions.

212

Hôtel Méridian-Montparnasse
1971-74
Pierre Dufau
19, Rue du Commandant-René-Mouchotte, 14e
Metro: Montparnasse-Bienvenue, Gaité

Built for the Sheraton chain, this dynamic hotel towers to 116 meters, with 31 floors, 950 rooms, and adroit terracing. Steel plates (painted white) and windows with aluminum frames conceal the concrete skeleton.

213
Forum des Halles
1973-79
Claude Vasconi and Georges Pencréac'h
Rue Pierre-Lescot, 1er
Metro: Les Halles

This site originally held the ten halls by Victor Baltard and Félix Callet, built after 1854 and achieving fame as the high point of 19th century glass-and-iron architecture (one was moved to Nogent-sur-Marne to serve as a cultural center). A richly-glassed and terraced crater by Claude Vasconi and Georges Pencréac'h was built in their place, opposed by a 20-meter high, megalomaniac concrete structure beneath Paul Chemetov's "Jardin des Halles" (1985).

214
Office Building
1976
Vittorio Mazzucconi
22, Avenue Matignon, 8e
Metro: Franklin-Roosevelt

Built in 1976 for the Thompson advertising agency, the blue glass façade of this office building integrates together various uneven classical ruins.

215
Australian Embassy
1978
Harry Seidler and Peter Hirst
4, Rue Jean-Rey, 15e
Metro: Bir-Hakeim

Built on a triangular, 6,300-square-meter plot with a first-rate view, this exterior-concrete building was built by Seidler and Hirst (consulted by Marcel Breuer, Pier Luigi Nervi, and Mario Jossa) from two quarter-arcs laid against each other. The seven-story office sits atop a tree-like support post with a stark relief effect from the rows of windows, bridges on the ground floor, and a nine-story residence section facing the Eiffel tower.

216
Totem Tower
1978
Pierre Parat and Michel Andrault
55, Quai de Grenelle, 15e
Metro: Dupleix

This high-rise of luxury apartments was built atop the "Front de Seine," a radical, new 12-hectare riverbank strip that once held old factories. Built with the motto "Exprimer le squelette, la structure: c'est ça l'architecture," each arm of the concrete scaffolding holds 6 three-story glass cubes for a grand total of 207 apartments.

217
Palais Omnisports de Paris-Bercy
1980-84
Jean Prouvé, Michel Andrault, Pierre Parat, and Aydin Guvan
8, Boulevard de Bercy, 12e
Metro: Bercy

This futuristic-looking, all-purpose arena encompasses 55,000 square meters of adaptable space that can hold from 3,500 to 17,000 visitors to a variety of events in its main hall. Andrault, Parat and Guvan built the capped, landscaped, 30-meter high pyramid whose walls tilt to 45 degrees. Four 6-meter thick and 30-meter high concrete columns hold up Jean Prouvé's blue glass ceiling construction.

218
"Place des Colonnes" Apartment Complex
1983-85
Ricardo Bofill
78, Rue du Château, 14e
Metro: Gaité

This monumental construction by Bofill, a Catalonian, corresponds to the neighboring Place de Catalogne. The seven-story apartment complex surrounds a grassy oval courtyard with colorful concrete imitation stones with chiseled ancient quotations.

219
Opéra de la Bastille
1982-89
Carlos Ott
2-8, Place de la Bastille, 12e
Metro: Bastille

President François Mitterand decided in 1982 that a new opera house was necessary, to be built on the site of the old Bastille train station of 1859. After an international design competition (750 entrants), Canadian Carlos Ott won the commission; the consecration took place in 1989 and the building opened in 1990. Although the attempt was made to tie the form of the plaza (a rounded façade) and the columns (stretching to 50 meters high), the link is questionable: the axis of the building is not to-wards the middle of the plaza, but rather to-wards the Sacré-Cœur. A freestanding staircase leads through a granite gateway, and the main staircase mirrors the façade, with colorful gradations of glass, steel, and stone. The 2,716 egalitarian seats of the main hall, whose materials and forms were created to fit the acoustical needs, swarm with black, gray, and blue tones. Similarly, the decor and decorations of the foyer and the three floors were dictated by the quadrant. Other facilities include a library, video library, amphitheater (500 seats), and a studio (246 seats) for musical films and concerts.

220
Institut du Monde Arabe
1982-87
Jean Nouvel
23, Quai St-Bernard, 5e
Metro: Cardinal Lemoine

This cultural center for the Arab world, was enabled by a treaty of 1980 between France and 19 Third World countries. Built according to plans by Nouvel, Henri Bernard, Pierre Soria, and Gilbert Lezendés, it features a curved, 25-meter high curtained façade with engraved outlines of the buildings on the river. Further back lay the screened library and media centers, illuminated by photo-electrically muted lights, as well as a book tower oriented towards the west.

221

Parc de La Villette
1982-89
Bernard Tschumi
211, Avenue Jean-Jaurès, 19e
Metro: Porte de Pantin

This amusement park, built on the 55-hectare site of the La Villette slaughterhouse, is, at 30 hectares, the largest in Paris. It is an amusement park in the modern sense, that is, as a "parc d'activités," not the 18th and 19th century sense more prevalent in Paris: there are few green expanses, but 60 thematic parks and around 30 "Folies," red metal cubes with 10 meter sides that serve a specific purpose, such as providing garden music. A 900-meter long covered gallery links sections of the plot's five large buildings above a canal. The oldest section is the "Grande Halle," which at 186×86 meters is the largest of the three former large animal

halls. The seven-aisle construction by Louis-Adolphe Janvier (1863-67) is one of the high points of glass-and-iron architecture, restored between 1983 and 1985 by Bernard Reichen and Philippe Robert. The "Cité des Sciences et de l'Industrie" is part exhibition, documentary, and communication center, housed in a gigantic hall (275×110×47 meter, 1964 by P.V. Fournier, J. Semichom, S. Waulan) that was renovated by Adrien Fainsilber from 1980-86 after a design competition (1980). It features an escalator connection between the exhibition floors, a glassed park front, and a water basin. The "La Géode" movie house is a sphere atop a huge concrete pillar (36 meter circumference), covered with 6,500 polished steel triangles. It was built by Fainsilber and Gérard Chamayou (1983-85). "Le Zénith" (75×75×12 meters) is a concert hall with 6,400 seats for rock and other performances. Built by Philippe Chaix and Jean P. Morel in 1983, the "salle de rock" on the Porte de Bagnolet was erected from removable steel pipes in only 12 months. It includes a 70-meter wide metal roof and a polyester two-layer exterior shell intended to last only 15 years. The "Cité de la Musique" remains unfinished. It is to be a two-part combination of a conservatory, musical instrument collection, and institute for musical instruction, built by Christian de Portzamparc.

222

Musée d'Orsay
1983-86
Team ACT and Gae Aulenti
9, Quai Anatole-France, 7e
Metro: Solférino

The Team ACT – P. Colboc, R. Bardon, J. P. Philippon – as well as Italian interior architect Gae Aulenti converted the main hall of the Gare d'Orsay into a 20,000 square meter museum of late 19th and early 20th century art. The two-story painting rooms, near a central sculptural axis, are designed to be linked through the numerous vantage points allowing visitors to see into different wings.

223

Grande Arche de la Défense
1989
Johann-Otto von Spreckelsen
Parvis de la Défense
Metro: La Défense

This open cube, built in 1989 according to the plans of von Spreckelsen, completed the long planned Louvre-Champs-Elysées-Défense axis, serving as a "window into the future." The monumental construction, planned to cover the plaza below (110 meter edges, 30 stories, 1 hectare of roof terrace space), is made of glass and Carrara marble and covers 15,000 square meters of floor space with its plinth. The tower offers 80,000 square meters of office space.

224

Economic and Financial Ministry
1988-89
Paul Chemetov and Borja Huidobro
1, Boulevard de Bercy, 12e
Metro: Bercy

This gigantic construction, built at a right angle to the Seine due to space constraints, resembles a viaduct: it is 360 meters long, but only 21 meters wide, serving up to 6,500 workers. One of its pairs of pillars even stands in the water. It was built to serve as an eastern entrance to the central part of the city and as replacement space for those displaced during the Louvre renovations.

225

Le "Grand Louvre"
1984-93
Ieoh Ming Pei
2, Place du Palais, 1er
Metro: Palais-Royal

The dedication of the Richelieu wing in 1993 signaled an important step in the complete renovation of the Louvre. After 15 years of reconstruction, several important departments of the museum – including the French painters, fine arts and craft work, and the sculpture collections – were finally moved to their new rooms. By roofing the three interior courtyards of the former finance ministry – Cour Marly, Cour Puget, and Cour Khorsabad, at 2,150, 1,800 and 520 square meters, respectively – with an outstanding glass construction, the architectural team of G. Duval, M. Macary, and Jean-Michel Wilmotte fulfilled Ieoh Ming Pei's (d. 1988) plans for expanded exhibition space, walkways, and lighting effects. Pei's glass pyramid became a landmark of the Grand Louvre, covering the new entrance hall in the lower floor of the complex, designed as a central staging area for the Denon, Sully, and Richelieu wings. As a counterpart to the glass roof, Pei planned a smaller pyramid to reach down into the lower floors, allowing natural light into this service area. Work on the Jardin du Carrousel and the Tuileries gardens, intended to create traditional "Jardin à la française," that is, geometric Renaissance gardens, has not yet been completed.

226

American Center
1994
Frank O. Gehry
51, Rue de Bercy, 12e
Metro: Bercy

In 1994 Californian Gehry completed the new American Center, a cultural institute founded in 1934 as a leisure club for Americans. The jumbled building rises from its tiny plot with numerous bay windows and a roof garden. Gehry took care to link the building with other historical Parisian buildings, including his façade of gold-colored sandstone and the zink roof covering. The "deconstructivist" attitude of the builder can be seen in the side facing the park.

227

Cartier-House
1994-95
Jean Nouvel
216, Boulevard Raspail, 14e
Metro: Raspail

Only opening in 1995, this building is the headquarters of the Fondation Cartier pour l'art contemporain, founded in 1984, who have 1,200 square meters of exhibition space on the ground and basement floors, and of Cartier France, who holds 4,000 square meters on 7 floors of offices. The plot once belonged to François René de Châteaubriand, whose cedar trees still grace the garden, and later the American Center. Behind a gigantic glass front in a freestanding steel frame which separates the building and the Theatrum Botanicum garden (by Düsseldorfer Lothar Baumgarten) from the loud boulevard, the glass building rises to 8 stories, using 650 tons of steel and 5,000 square meters of glass. Its longer sides lengthen the freestanding glass surfaces. Employing large transparencies, extensive dematerialization, and multiple light and visual effects, Nouvel sought to distinguish his "architecture de toute légèreté" theory.

228

Bibliothèque de France
1991-95
Dominique Perrault
13, Quai Panhard-Levassor, 13e
Metro: Bercy

Dedicated in 1995 but not yet opened, this new National Library is one part of the renovation of the Seine-Rive Gauche district, a 130-hectare area in the Tolbiac quarter. The four 80-meter towers of glass and steel with 25 stories, designed in an L-form, build the corners of a 375×260 rectangle. The garden is surrounded by reading rooms with 4,000 work cubicles and space for 850,000 open stack books. Stacks for 10,000,000 books reside in the towers.

Bibliography

1936

M. DUMOLIN, MAURICE and G. OUTARDEL, Les églises de France: Paris et la Seine, Paris.

1942

R. HÉRON DE VILLEFOSSE, Prés et bois parisiens, Paris.

1945

P. JARRY, Vieilles demeures parisiennes, Paris.

1947

Y. CHRIST, Eglises parisiennes actuelles et disparues, Paris.

1953

J. HILLAIRET, Evocation du vieux Paris: les faubourgs, Paris.

1956

J. HILLAIRET, Connaissance du vieux Paris, Paris.

1957

G. POISSON, Fontaines de Paris, Paris.

1958

A. BOINET, Les églises parisiennes, Paris.
J. HILLAIRET, Les 200 cimetières du vieux Paris, Paris.

1960

P.M. DUVAL, Paris antique, des origines au troisième siècle, Paris.
G. POISSON, Evocation du grand Paris: la banlieu nord-ouest, Paris.

1961

M. VIEILLARD-TROIEKOUROFF et al., Les églises suburbaines de Paris du IVe au Xe siècle, Paris.

1963

M.L. BIVER, Le Paris de Napoléon, Paris.

1964

M. GALLET, Demeures parisiennes — L'époque de Louis XVI, Paris.
G. POISSON, Napoléon et Paris, Paris.

1965

J.P. BABELON, Demeures parisiennes sous Henri IV et Louis XIII, Paris.

1967

J. and B. BEAUJEU-GARNIER, Atlas de Paris, Paris.
R. PLOUIN, Les ponts de Paris, Paris.
E. SCHILD, Zwischen Glaspalast und Palais des Illusions, Berlin.

1968

P. COUPERIE, Paris au fil du temps, atlas historique, Paris.

1969

R.H. GUERRAND, Les origines du logement social en France, Paris.

1970

C. BEUTLER, Paris und Versailles, Stuttgart.
M.L. and P. BIVER, Abbayes, monastères et couvents de Paris, Paris.
J.F. BOSHER, French Finances 1770-1795, Cambridge.
Y. CHRIST, Paris des utopies, Paris.
H. ROSENAU, Social Purpose in Architecture: Paris and London Compared 1760-1800, London.

A. SUTCLIFFE, The Autumn of Central Paris — The Defeat of Town Planning 1850-1970, London.
J. TULARD, Le Consulat et l'Empire 1800-1815, Paris.

1971

M. EMERY, Un siècle d'architecture moderne, Paris.
M.R. REINHARD, La Révolution (1789-1799), Paris.
H. SAALMAN, Haussmann: Paris Transformed, New York.

1972

R. CAZELLES, Paris de la fin du règne de Philippe Auguste à la mort de Charles V, 1223-1380, Paris.
P.M. DUVAL, Résumé du Paris antique, Paris.
M. GALLET, Paris Domestic Architecture, London.
W.G. KALNEIN and M. LEVEY, Art and Architecture of the 18th Century in France, Harmondsworth.
D.H. PINKNEY, Napoleon III and the Rebuilding of Paris, Princeton.

1973

B. CHAMPIGNEULLE, Paris — Architectures, sites & jardins, Paris.
G. ROISECCO, L'architettura del ferro: la Francia (1715-1914), Rome.

1974

J. FAVIER, Paris au XVe siècle, Paris.
M. FLEURY et al., Paris, Munich.

1975

M.L. and P. BIVER, Abbayes, monastères et couvents de femmes à Paris, Paris.

P. LAVEDAN, Histoire de l'urbanisme à Paris, Paris.

B. ROULEAU, Le Tracé des Rues de Paris, Paris.

1976

J. BOUSSARD, De la fin du siège de 885 886 à la mort de Philippe Auguste, Paris.

P. CHEMETOV and BERNARD MARREY, Familièrement inconnues ... architectures à Paris 1848-1914, Paris.

Y. CHRIST, Les nouvelles métamorphoses de Paris, Paris.

A. LOMBARD-JOURDAN, Paris, genèse de la ville, Paris.

R. MOUSNIER, La stratification sociale à Paris aux XVIIe et XVIIIe siècles, Paris.

G. PILLEMENT, Du Paris des rois au Paris des promoteurs, Paris.

1977

G. DE BERTIER DE SAUVIGNY, La Restauration (1815-1830), Paris.

F. BOUDON et al., Le Quartier des Halles à Paris, Paris.

P. LAVEDAN, Histoire de Paris, Paris.

Jardins en France 1760-1820, Paris.

1978

De Bagatelle à Monceau 1778-1978. Les folies du XVIIIe siècle à Paris, Paris.

R. MOUSNIER, Paris capitale au temps de Richelieu et de Mazarin, Paris.

1979

De Belleville à Charonne, Paris.

J. HILLAIRET, Dictionnaire des rues de Paris, Paris.

B. MARREY, Les grands magasins des origines à 1939, Paris.

1980

A. BRAHAM, The Architecture of French Enlightenment, Berkeley and Los Angeles.

D.D. EGBERT, The Beaux-Arts Tradition in French Architecture, Princeton.

R. HÉRON DE VILLEFOSSE, Solennités, fêtes et réjouissances parisiennes, Paris.

La Rue de Grenelle, Paris.

Paris Mérovingien, Paris.

1980

M. RACHLINE, Paris et ses peintres, Paris.

1981

J.C. DELORME et al., L'Ecole de Paris, dix architectes et leurs immeubles, Paris.

M. GAILLARD, Paris au XIX siècle, Paris.

L. GIRARD, La 1ère République et le second Empire (1848-1870), Paris.

Ile Saint-Louis, Paris.

La Rue de Varenne, Paris.

La Montagne Sainte-Geneviève, Paris.

1982

De la place Louis XV à la place de la Concorde, Paris.

Childéric-Clovis — Rois des Francs 482-1983, Tournai.

Chaillot, Passy, Auteuil, Paris.

D. KIMPEL, Paris — Führer durch die Stadtbaugeschichte, Munich.

R. MIDDLETON, The Beaux Arts and the 19th-Century French Architecture, London.

1983

B.B. DIEFENDORF, Paris City Councillors in the 16th Century, Princeton.

Du faubourg Saint-Antoine au bois de Vincennes, Paris.

N. EVENSON, Paris, cent ans de travaux et d'urbanisme 1878-1978, Paris.

A. GRIMAULT and M. FLEURY, Anciennes enceintes et limites de Paris, Paris.

La Rue de Lille. L'Hôtel de Salm, Paris.

1984

De Vaugirard à Grenelle, Paris.

R.A. ETLIN, The Architecture of Death — The Transformation of the Cemetery in the 18th Century, Paris and Cambridge.

J. DE FONTGALLAND et al., Le Louvre et son quartier. 800 ans d'histoire architecturale, Paris.

Le XVIe arrondissement: Mécène de l'art nouveau 1895-1914, Paris.

La Rue Saint-Dominique. Hôtels et Amateurs, Paris.

La Nouvelle Athènes, Paris.

Lutèce — Paris de César à Clovis, Paris.

D. THOMSON, Renaissance Paris, Architecture and Growth 1475-1600, London.

1985

R. CAMERON, Au-dessus de Paris. Un album de vues aériennes, Paris.

F. CHASLIN, Le Paris de François Mitterrand, Histoire des grands projets architecturaux, Paris.

Du faubourg Saint-Antoine au faubourg du Temple, Paris.

Les Grands Boulevards, Paris.

Paris et son Université, Paris.

S. RIALS, De Trochu à Thiers (1870-1873), Paris.

M. ROBLIN, Quand Paris était à la campagne, Paris.

B. ROULEAU, Villages et faubourgs de l'ancien Paris, Paris.

Saint-Paul — Saint-Louis. Les jésuites à Paris, Paris.

1986

J.P. BABELON, Paris au XVIe siècle, Paris.

De Montparnasse à Montsouris, Paris.

M. DENNIS, Court & Garden. From the French Hôtel to the City of Modern Architecture, Cambridge.

Des Ternes aux Batignolles, Paris.

Le Faubourg Poissonnière: Architecture, élégance et décor, Paris.

1987

A. and Y. ARTHUR BERTRAND, Paris vu du ciel, Paris.

J. DE BRUNHOFF, La place Dauphi-

ne et l'Ile de la Cité, Paris.
A. CHAZELLES, Paris vu par les peintres, Lausanne.
J. C. DELORME and S. COUTURIER, Les villas d'artistes à Paris, Paris.
J.C. GARRETTA, L'Ile de la Cité, Paris.
La Chartreuse de Paris, Paris.
Le Marais. Mythe et réalité, Paris.
B. LEMOINE and P. RIVOIRARD, Paris. L'architecture des années trente, Lyon.
Les grandes gares parisiennes du XIXe siècle, Paris.
F. LOYER, Paris XIXe siècle. L'immeuble et la rue, Paris.
H. MARTIN, Guide de l'architecture moderne à Paris 1900-1990, Paris.
Palais Bourbon, sa place, Paris.
Paris 1937 Cinquantenaire, Paris.
Paris 1937. L'art indépendant, Paris.
Rue de l'Université, Paris.
D. VAN ZANTEN, Designing Paris – The Architecture of Duban, Labrouste, Duc and Vaudoyer, Cambridge.

1988
J. CHAGNIOT, Paris au XVIII siècle, Paris.
Y. CHRIST et al., Vie et histoire des arrondissements, Paris.
Les Champs-Elysées et leur quartier, Paris.
R. PILLORGET, Paris sous les premiers Bourbons, Paris.
J. WILLMS, Paris. Hauptstadt Europas 1789-1914, Munich.

1989
E.J. BIASINI (ed.), Architecture Capitales – Paris 1979-1989, Paris, 1992².
P. CHEMETOV et al., Paris-Banlieue 1919-1939. Architectures domestiques, Paris.
K. FEIREISS, Paris – Architektur und Utopie. Städtebauliche Entwürfe für den Aufbruch in das 21. Jahrhundert, Berlin.
Les Traversées de Paris. Deux siècles de révolutions dans la ville, Paris.
A. LOMBARD-JOURDAN, Montjoie et Saint-Denis. Le centre de la Gaule aux origines de Paris et de Saint-Denis, Paris.
B. MARREY, Le Fer à Paris. Architectures, Paris.

1990
F. BORSI and E. GODOLI, Pariser Bauten der Jahrhundertwende, Stuttgart.
J.P. COURTIAU, Pari. Un siècle de fantasmes architecturaux et de projets faux, Paris.
G. DETHAN, Paris sous Louis XIV, Paris.
J. FRIEDMAN, Interieurs in Paris, Munich.
M. KAMPMEYER-KÄDING, Paris unter dem Zweiten Kaiserreich, Marburg.
La Rue du Bac, Paris.
Le Quai Voltaire, Paris.
M. LE MOEL, L'architecture privée à Paris au grand siècle, Paris.
G. ROUSSET-CHARNY, Les palais parisiens de la Belle Epoque, Paris.
Sous les pavés. La Bastille, Paris.

1991
H. BALLON, The Paris of Henri IV. Architecture and Urbanism, Cambridge and London.
E. GÉRARDS, Paris souterrain, Paris.
H.A. JAHN, Das neue Paris, Dortmund.
P. DE MONCAN and C. MAHOUT, Le Paris du Baron Haussmann, Paris.
Paris – Haussmann. "Le Paris d'Haussmann", Paris.
P. VIGIER, Paris pendant la Monarchie de Juillet, Paris.

1992
J. COLSON and M.C. LAUROA, Dictionnaire des monuments de Paris, Paris.
De la Rue des Colonnes à la Rue de Rivoli, Paris.
A. DOMENECH, Les grands travaux à Paris, Paris.
R. GARGIANI, Paris. Architektur zwischen Purismus und Beaux-Arts 1919-1939, Braunschweig.
La Rue des Francs-Bourgeois, Paris.
Les Ordres mendiants à Paris, Paris.
J. LUCAN, Eau et gaz à tous les étages. Paris, 100 ans de logement, Paris.
P. PETERS, Paris. Die Großen Projekte, Berlin.
J.F. PINCHON, Les Palais d'Argent, Paris.
P. VELAY, From Lutetia to Paris. The Island and the Two Banks, Paris.

1993
F. FERRÉ, Paris. Architecture contemporaine: 1955-95, Paris.
J.R. PITTE et al., Paris. Histoire d'une Ville, Paris.
A. SUTCLIFFE, Paris: An Architectural History, New Haven.

1994
B. MARREY, Le brique à Paris, Paris.
A. MCCLELLAN, Inventing the Louvre. Art, Politics and the Origin of the Modern Museum in the 18th Century, Paris and Cambridge.
Paris – Belle Epoque 1880-1914, Faszination einer Weltstadt, Essen.
Paris de l'Antiquité à nos jours, Paris.
A.S. POTOFSKY, The Builders of Modern Paris. The Organization of Labor from Turgot to Napoleon, New York (Dissertation).
Rue du Faubourg-Saint-Honoré, Paris.
F. SEITZ, Architecture et métal en France, 19e et 20e siècle, Paris.
N. SILVER, The Making of Beaubourg, Cambridge.
D. VAN ZANTEN, Building Paris. Architectural Institutions and the Transformation of the French Capital, 1830-1870, Cambridge.

1995
B. MARREY, Les ponts modernes: 20e siècle, Paris.
Paris d'Ingénieurs, Paris.

Index of places

The names in small capital letters refer to those buildings covered at length in this guide book..
The **boldface** numbers refer to the numbering of the files, not the page number.

Index of names

Q

Quatremère de Quincy, Antoine
Chrysostome 53, 80

R

Récipon, Georges 108
Regnaudin, Thomas 62
Régnier de Guerchy, Louis 58
Reichen, Bernard 134
Résal, Jean 109
Richelieu (Cardinal) 14, 41, 46,
52, 55, 57, 58
Robert, Philippe 134
Rochechouart (Comtesse de) 90
Rodin, François-Auguste-René 73
Rogers, Richard 130
Rohan, Armand G. Max de (Bi-
shop) 68
Rohan, François de (Prince of
Soubise) 68
Rohault de Fleury, Charles 96
Rohault de Fleury, Hubert 87
Roland, Philippe-Laurent 51, 94
Rondelet, Jean-Baptiste 80
Roquelaure, Antoine Gaston de
(Duke) 72
Rothschild (Family) 60
Rothschild, Edmond de (Baron)
100
Rousseau, Pierre 79, 94
Roux-Spitz, Michel 59, 122
Rubens, Peter-Paul 57
Rude, François 98

S

Salazar, Tristan de (Archibishop
of Sens) 39
Saubat, Jean 129
Saubot, Roger 126
Sauvage, Henri 117, 120
Sédille, Paul 58
Seidler, Harry 131
Semichom, J. 134
Sens (Bishop from) 27
Servandoni, Giovanni Niccolò 48
Severino (Settler) 26
Sévigné, Madame de 53
Singer, Winaretta (Princess of
Polignac) 122
Skidmore, Owings and Merrill
126
Slodtz, Michel-Ange 48
Sorbon, Robert de 46
Soria, Pierre 133
Soufflot, Jacques Germain 80
Spreckelsen, Johann-Otto von 135
Stenzel, Michel 126
Strom, J.B. 85
Sully (Duke of) 14, 69
Sully, Maurice de (Bishop) 23, 28

T

Taillibert, Roger 21, 129
Tallard (Count of) 62

Team ACT (P. Colboc, R. Bar-
don, J.P. Philippon) 109, 135
Terrat, Jean Gaston Baptiste
(Marquis de Chantosme) 67
Thiers, Adolphe (Minister) 18,
98
Thiriot, Jean 59
Thiroux de Montsauge 91
Thoix (Marquise de) 70
Thomas, Albert 108
Tillet, Charles du (Marquis de La
Bussière) 75
Tour d'Auvergne, Henri Louis de
la 69
Tournaire, Albert 38
Tournon, Paul 113
Tours, Gregor of 12, 29
Trémoille, Antoine-François de la
(Duke of Noirmoutiers) 70
Triqueti, Henri de 81
Tschumi, Bernard 134
Tuby, Jean-Baptiste 51
Tureau, Jean-Bernard 75
Tzara, Tristan 119

U

Uchard, Joseph 86

V

Valois, Marguerite de 101
Van de Velde, Henry 117
Vasconi, Claude 131
Vaudremer, Joseph 107
Vautrain, Jean-Baptiste 75
Vellefaux, Claude 56
Vernet, Horace 71
Verniquet, Edme 16, 96
Verton, Pierre de (Secretary of
State) 72
Viard 124
Vignon, Pierre A. 81
Vigny, Pierre de 72
Viguier, Etienne 33
Vincent of Paola (S.) 84
Viollet-le-Duc, Eugène 18, 107
Visconti, Louis T.J. 35, 48, 52,
100
Vitry, Bernard de 61
Volterra, Daniele da 55
Vouet, Simon 69

W

Wailly, Charles de 91
Wassiliew, Joseph 85
Waulan, S. 134
Wilmotte, Jean-Michel 136

Z

Zehrfuss, Bernard 126, 128
Ziegler, Jules 81